LEVITICUS

The Third Book of Moses

This **WORKBOOK** is designed to help assist the diligent study of those who would know the Word of God. It is written in a format that REQUIRES reading of the text from the Authorized King James Version of the Holy Scriptures.

The King James Bible correctly fills all of the available "blanks" in this workbook.

Other workbooks are available by contacting us:

By FAITH Publications
85 Hendersonville Hwy.
Walterboro, SC 29488

(843) 538-2269

www.faithbaptistchurch.us

publications@faithbaptistchurch.us

LEVITICUS

Leviticus 1:1-27:34 (KJV)

And the Lord called unto _____, and spake unto him out of the tabernacle of the congregation, saying, [2] Speak unto the children of Israel, and say unto them, If any man of you bring an _____ unto the Lord, ye shall bring your _____ of the cattle, even of the herd, and of the flock. [3] If his offering be a burnt sacrifice of the herd, let him offer a male without _____ : he shall offer it of his own _____ _____ at the door of the tabernacle of the congregation before the Lord. [4] And he shall put his hand upon the head of the burnt offering; and it shall be accepted for him to make atonement for him. [5] And he shall kill the bullock before the Lord: and the priests, Aaron's sons, shall bring the blood, and sprinkle the blood round about upon the altar that is by the door of the tabernacle of the congregation. [6] And he shall flay the burnt offering, and cut it into his pieces. [7] And the sons of Aaron the priest shall put fire upon the altar, and lay the wood in order upon the fire: [8] And the priests, Aaron's sons, shall lay the parts, the head, and the fat, in order upon the wood that is on the fire which is upon the altar: [9] But his inwards and his legs shall he wash in water: and the priest shall burn all on the altar, to be a burnt sacrifice, an offering made by fire, of a sweet savour unto the _____ .

[10] And if his offering be of the _____ , namely, of the sheep, or of the goats, for a burnt sacrifice; he shall bring it a male without blemish. [11] And he shall kill it on the side of the altar northward before the Lord: and the priests, Aaron's sons, shall sprinkle his blood round about upon the altar. [12] And he shall cut it into his pieces, with his head and his fat: and the priest shall lay them in order on the wood that is on the fire which is upon the altar: [13] But he shall wash the inwards and the legs with water: and the priest shall bring it all, and burn it upon the altar: it is a burnt sacrifice, an offering made by fire, of a sweet savour unto the Lord.

[14] And if the burnt sacrifice for his offering to the Lord be of _____ , then he shall bring his offering of turtledoves, or of young pigeons. [15] And the priest shall bring it unto the altar, and wring off his head, and burn it on the altar; and the blood thereof shall be wrung out at the side of the altar: [16] And he shall pluck away his crop with his feathers, and cast it beside the altar on the east part, by the place of the ashes: [17] And he shall cleave it with the wings thereof, but shall not divide it asunder: and the priest shall burn it upon the altar, upon the wood that is upon the fire: it is a burnt sacrifice, an offering made by fire, of a sweet savour unto the Lord.

[2:1] And when any will offer a _____ offering unto the Lord, his offering shall be of fine flour; and he shall pour _____ upon it, and put _____ thereon: [2] And he shall bring it to Aaron's sons the priests: and he shall take thereout his handful of the flour thereof, and of the oil thereof, with all the frankincense thereof; and the priest shall burn the memorial of it upon the altar, to be an offering made by fire, of a sweet savour unto the Lord: [3] And the _____ of the meat offerings shall be _____ and his _____ : it is a thing most _____ of the offerings of the Lord made by fire.

[4] And if thou bring an oblation of a meat offering baken in the oven, it shall be _____ cakes of fine flour mingled with _____ , or _____ wafers anointed with _____ .

[5] And if thy oblation be a meat offering baken in a pan, it shall be of fine flour _____, mingled with _____. [6] Thou shalt part it in pieces, and pour oil thereon: it is a meat offering.

[7] And if thy oblation be a meat offering baken in the _____ pan, it shall be made of fine flour with oil. [8] And thou shalt bring the meat offering that is made of these things unto the Lord: and when it is presented unto the priest, he shall bring it unto the altar. [9] And the priest shall take from the meat offering a memorial thereof, and shall burn it upon the altar: it is an offering made by fire, of a sweet savour unto the Lord. [10] And that which is left of the meat offering shall be Aaron's and his sons': it is a thing most holy of the offerings of the Lord made by fire. [11] _____ meat offering, which ye shall bring unto the Lord, shall be made with _____: for ye shall burn no leaven, nor any _____, in any offering of the Lord made by fire.

[12] As for the oblation of the _____, ye shall offer them unto the Lord: but they shall not be burnt on the altar for a sweet savour. [13] And every oblation of thy meat offering shalt thou season with _____; neither shalt thou suffer the salt of the covenant of thy God to be lacking from thy meat offering: with all thine offerings thou shalt offer salt. [14] And if thou offer a meat offering of thy firstfruits unto the Lord, thou shalt offer for the meat offering of thy firstfruits green ears of corn dried by the fire, even corn beaten out of full ears. [15] And thou shalt put oil upon it, and lay frankincense thereon: it is a meat offering. [16] And the priest shall burn the memorial of it, part of the beaten corn thereof, and part of the oil thereof, with all the frankincense thereof: it is an offering made by fire unto the Lord.

[3:1] And if his oblation be a sacrifice of _____ offering, if he offer it of the herd; whether it be a male or female, he shall offer it without _____ before the Lord. [2] And he shall lay his hand upon the _____ of his offering, and _____ it at the door of the tabernacle of the congregation: and Aaron's sons the priests shall sprinkle the _____ upon the altar round about. [3] And he shall offer of the sacrifice of the peace offering an offering made by fire unto the Lord; the fat that covereth the inwards, and all the fat that is upon the inwards, [4] And the two kidneys, and the fat that is on them, which is by the flanks, and the caul above the liver, with the kidneys, it shall he take away. [5] And Aaron's sons shall burn it on the altar upon the burnt sacrifice, which is upon the wood that is on the fire: it is an offering made by fire, of a sweet savour unto the Lord.

[6] And if his offering for a sacrifice of peace offering unto the Lord be of the flock; male or female, he shall offer it without blemish. [7] If he offer a lamb for his offering, then shall he offer it before the Lord. [8] And he shall lay his hand upon the head of his offering, and kill it before the tabernacle of the congregation: and Aaron's sons shall sprinkle the blood thereof round about upon the altar. [9] And he shall offer of the sacrifice of the peace offering an offering made by fire unto the Lord; the fat thereof, and the whole rump, it shall he take off hard by the backbone; and the fat that covereth the inwards, and all the fat that is upon the inwards, [10] And the two kidneys, and the fat that is upon them, which is by the flanks, and the caul above the liver, with the kidneys, it shall he take away. [11] And the priest shall burn it upon the altar: it is the food of the offering made by fire unto the Lord.

[12] And if his offering be a _____, then he shall offer it before the Lord. [13] And he shall lay his hand upon the head of it, and kill it before the tabernacle of the

LEVICUS

congregation: and the sons of Aaron shall sprinkle the blood thereof upon the altar round about. [14] And he shall offer thereof his offering, even an offering made by fire unto the Lord; the fat that covereth the inwards, and all the fat that is upon the inwards, [15] And the two kidneys, and the fat that is upon them, which is by the flanks, and the caul above the liver, with the kidneys, it shall he take away. [16] And the priest shall burn them upon the altar: it is the food of the offering made by fire for a sweet savour: all the fat is the Lord's. [17] It shall be a perpetual _____ for your generations throughout all your dwellings, that ye _____ neither _____ nor _____.

[4:1] And the Lord spake unto Moses, saying, [2] Speak unto the children of Israel, saying, If a soul shall _____ through _____ against any of the commandments of the Lord concerning things which ought _____to be done, and shall do against any of them: [3] If the priest that is anointed do sin according to the sin of the people; then let him bring for his sin, which he hath sinned, a young _____without blemish unto the Lord for a sin offering. [4] And he shall bring the bullock unto the door of the tabernacle of the congregation before the Lord; and shall lay his hand upon the bullock's head, and kill the bullock before the Lord. [5] And the priest that is anointed shall take of the bullock's blood, and bring it to the tabernacle of the congregation: [6] And the _____shall dip his finger in the _____, and sprinkle of the blood _____times before the Lord, before the vail of the sanctuary. [7] And the priest shall put some of the blood upon the _____of the altar of sweet incense before the Lord, which is in the tabernacle of the congregation: and shall pour all the blood of the bullock at the bottom of the altar of the burnt offering, which is at the door of the tabernacle of the congregation. [8] And he shall take off from it all the fat of the bullock for the sin offering; the fat that covereth the inwards, and all the fat that is upon the inwards, [9] And the two kidneys, and the fat that is upon them, which is by the flanks, and the caul above the liver, with the kidneys, it shall he take away, [10] As it was taken off from the bullock of the sacrifice of peace offerings: and the priest shall burn them upon the altar of the burnt offering. [11] And the _____of the bullock, and all his flesh, with his head, and with his legs, and his inwards, and his dung, [12] Even the whole bullock shall he carry forth without the camp unto a clean place, where the ashes are poured out, and burn him on the wood with fire: where the ashes are poured out shall he be burnt.

[13] And if the whole congregation of Israel _____through _____, and the thing be hid from the eyes of the assembly, and they have done somewhat against any of the commandments of the Lord concerning things which should not be done, and are _____; [14] When the sin, which they have sinned against it, is known, then the congregation shall offer a young bullock for the sin, and bring him before the tabernacle of the congregation. [15] And the elders of the congregation shall lay their hands upon the head of the bullock before the Lord: and the bullock shall be killed before the Lord. [16] And the _____that is _____shall bring of the bullock's blood to the tabernacle of the congregation: [17] And the priest shall dip his finger in some of the blood, and sprinkle it _____times before the Lord, even _____the _____. [18] And he shall put some of the blood upon the _____of the _____which is before the Lord, that is in the tabernacle of the congregation, and shall pour out all the blood at the bottom of the altar of the burnt offering, which is at the door of the tabernacle of the congregation. [19] And he shall take all his fat from him,

and burn it upon the altar. [20] And he shall do with the bullock as he did with the bullock for a sin offering, so shall he do with this: and the priest shall make an _____ for them, and it shall be _____ them. [21] And he shall carry forth the bullock without the camp, and burn him as he burned the first bullock: it is a sin offering for the congregation.

[22] When a _____ hath _____, and done somewhat through _____ against any of the commandments of the Lord his God concerning things which should not be done, and is _____; [23] Or if his sin, wherein he hath sinned, come to his _____; he shall bring his offering, a _____ of the goats, a _____ without _____: [24] And he shall lay his hand upon the head of the goat, and kill it in the place where they kill the burnt offering before the Lord: it is a sin offering. [25] And the _____ shall take of the _____ of the sin offering with his finger, and put it upon the horns of the altar of burnt offering, and shall pour out his blood at the bottom of the altar of burnt offering. [26] And he shall burn all his fat upon the altar, as the fat of the sacrifice of peace offerings: and the priest shall make an atonement for him as concerning his _____, and it shall be _____ him.

[27] And if any one of the _____ people sin through _____, while he doeth somewhat against any of the commandments of the Lord concerning things which ought not to be done, and be guilty; [28] Or if his sin, which he hath sinned, come to his knowledge: then he shall bring his offering, a kid of the goats, a _____ without blemish, for his sin which he hath sinned. [29] And he shall lay his hand upon the head of the sin offering, and _____ the sin offering in the place of the burnt offering. [30] And the priest shall take of the blood thereof with his finger, and put it upon the horns of the altar of burnt offering, and shall pour out all the blood thereof at the bottom of the altar. [31] And he shall take away all the fat thereof, as the fat is taken away from off the sacrifice of peace offerings; and the priest shall burn it upon the altar for a sweet savour unto the Lord; and the priest shall make an _____ for him, and it shall be _____ him. [32] And if he bring a _____ for a sin offering, he shall bring it a female without blemish. [33] And he shall lay his hand upon the head of the sin offering, and slay it for a sin offering in the place where they kill the burnt offering [34] And the priest shall take of the blood of the sin offering with his finger, and put it upon the horns of the altar of burnt offering, and shall pour out all the blood thereof at the bottom of the altar: [35] And he shall take away all the fat thereof, as the fat of the lamb is taken away from the sacrifice of the peace offerings; and the priest shall burn them upon the altar, according to the offerings made by fire unto the Lord: and the priest shall make an atonement for his sin that he hath committed, and it shall be _____ him.

[5:1] And if a _____ sin, and _____ the _____ of _____, and is a _____, whether he hath _____ or _____ of it; if he do _____ _____ it, then he shall bear his iniquity. [2] Or if a soul _____ any _____ thing, whether it be a carcase of an unclean beast, or a carcase of unclean cattle, or the carcase of unclean creeping things, and if it be hidden from him; he also shall be _____, and _____. [3] Or if he touch the uncleanness of man, whatsoever uncleanness it be that a man shall be defiled withal, and it be hid from him; _____ he knoweth of it, then he shall be _____. [4] Or if a soul _____, pronouncing with his lips to do _____, or to do good, whatsoever it be that a man shall pronounce with an _____, and it be hid from him; when he knoweth of it, then he shall be guilty in one of these. [5] And it shall be, when he shall be guilty in one of these things, that he shall _____ that he hath _____ in that thing: [6] And he shall bring his trespass offering unto the Lord for his sin which he hath sinned, a female from the flock, a lamb or a kid of the goats, for a sin offering; and the priest shall make an atonement for him concerning his sin. [7] And if he be _____ able to bring a lamb, then he shall bring for his trespass, which he hath committed, two turtledoves, or two young pigeons, unto the Lord; one for a _____ offering, and the other for a burnt offering. [8] And he shall bring them unto the priest, who shall offer that which is for the sin offering first, and wring off his head from his neck, but shall not divide it asunder: [9] And he shall sprinkle of the blood of the sin offering upon the side of the altar; and the rest of the blood shall be wrung out at the bottom of the altar: it is a sin offering. [10] And he shall offer the second for a burnt offering, according to the manner: and the priest shall make an atonement for him for his sin which he hath sinned, and it shall be _____ him.

[11] But if he be not able to bring two turtledoves, or two young pigeons, then he that sinned shall bring for his offering the tenth part of an ephah of fine flour for a sin offering; he shall put no _____ upon it, neither shall he put any _____ thereon: for it is a _____ offering. [12] Then shall he bring it to the priest, and the priest shall take his handful of it, even a memorial thereof, and burn it on the altar, according to the offerings made by fire unto the Lord: it is a sin offering. [13] And the priest shall make an atonement for him as touching his sin that he hath sinned in one of these, and it shall be forgiven him: and the _____ shall be the _____, as a _____ offering.

[14] And the Lord spake unto Moses, saying, [15] If a soul commit a _____, and sin through _____, in the _____ things of the Lord; then he shall bring for his trespass unto the Lord a ram without blemish out of the flocks, with thy estimation by shekels of silver, after the shekel of the sanctuary, for a trespass offering: [16] And he shall make _____ for the _____ that he hath done in the holy thing, and shall _____ the _____ part thereto, and give it unto the priest: and the priest shall make an atonement for him with the ram of the trespass offering, and it shall be forgiven him.

[17] And if a soul sin, and commit any of these things which are forbidden to be done by the commandments of the Lord; though he wist it not, yet is he guilty, and shall bear his iniquity. [18] And he shall bring a ram without blemish out of the flock, with thy estimation, for a trespass offering, unto the priest: and the priest shall make an atonement for him concerning his ignorance wherein he erred and wist it not, and it shall be forgiven him. [19] It is a trespass offering: he hath certainly trespassed against the Lord.

[6:1] And the Lord spake unto Moses, saying, [2] If a soul sin, and commit a trespass against the Lord, and _____ unto his neighbour in that which was delivered him to keep, or in fellowship, or in a thing taken away by violence, or hath deceived his neighbour; [3] Or have found that which was _____, and _____ concerning it, and _____ falsely; in any of all these that a man doeth, sinning therein: [4] Then it shall be, because he hath sinned, and is guilty, that he shall restore that which he took violently away, or the thing which he hath deceitfully gotten, or that which was delivered him to keep, or the lost thing which he found, [5] Or all that about which he hath sworn falsely; he shall even _____ it in the _____, and shall _____ the _____part more thereto, and give it unto him to whom it appertaineth, in the day of his trespass offering. [6] And he shall bring his trespass offering unto the Lord, a ram without _____out of the flock, with thy estimation, for a trespass offering, unto the _____: [7] And the priest shall make an _____for him before the Lord: and it shall be _____him for any thing of all that he hath done in trespassing therein.

[8] And the Lord spake unto Moses, saying, [9] Command _____and his sons, saying, This is the _____of the burnt offering: It is the burnt offering, because of the burning upon the altar all _____unto the morning, and the fire of the altar shall be burning in it. [10] And the priest shall put on his linen garment, and his linen breeches shall he put upon his flesh, and take up the ashes which the fire hath consumed with the burnt offering on the altar, and he shall put them _____the altar. [11] And he shall put off his garments, and put on other garments, and carry forth the ashes without the camp unto a _____place. [12] And the fire upon the altar shall be burning in it; it shall _____be put out: and the priest shall burn wood on it every morning, and lay the burnt offering in order upon it; and he shall burn thereon the fat of the peace offerings. [13] The fire shall ever be burning upon the altar; it shall _____go out.

[14] And this is the law of the meat offering: the sons of Aaron shall offer it before the Lord, before the altar. [15] And he shall take of it his _____, of the flour of the meat offering, and of the oil thereof, and all the frankincense which is upon the meat offering, and shall burn it upon the altar for a sweet _____, even the _____of it, unto the Lord. [16] And the remainder thereof shall Aaron and his sons _____: with unleavened bread shall it be eaten in the holy place; in the court of the tabernacle of the congregation they shall eat it. [17] It shall not be baken with _____. I have given it unto them for their portion of my offerings made by fire; it is most _____, as is the sin offering, and as the trespass offering. [18] All the males among the children of Aaron shall eat of it. It shall be a statute for ever in your generations concerning the offerings of the Lord made by fire: every one that toucheth them shall be holy.

[19] And the Lord spake unto Moses, saying, [20] This is the offering of Aaron and of his sons, which they shall offer unto the Lord in the day when he is anointed; the tenth part of an ephah of fine flour for a meat offering perpetual, half of it in the morning, and half thereof at night. [21] In a _____it shall be made with oil; and when it is baken, thou shalt bring it in: and the baken pieces of the meat offering shalt thou offer for a sweet savour unto the Lord. [22] And the priest of his sons that is anointed in his stead shall offer it: it is a statute for ever unto the Lord, it shall be wholly burnt. [23] For every meat offering for the priest shall be wholly burnt: it shall not be eaten.

[24] And the Lord spake unto Moses, saying, [25] Speak unto Aaron and to his sons, saying, This is the law of the sin offering: In the place where the _____offering is killed shall the _____offering be killed before the Lord: it is most holy. [26] The priest that offereth it for sin shall eat it: in the holy place shall it be eaten, in the court of the tabernacle of the congregation. [27] Whatsoever shall touch the flesh thereof shall be holy: and when there is sprinkled of the blood thereof upon any garment, thou shalt wash that whereon it was sprinkled in the holy place. [28] But the earthen vessel wherein it is sodden shall be broken: and if it be sodden in a brasen pot, it shall be both scoured, and rinsed in water. [29] All the males among the priests shall eat thereof: it is most holy.

[30] And no sin offering, whereof any of the blood is brought into the tabernacle of the congregation to reconcile withal in the holy place, shall be eaten: it shall be burnt in the fire.

[7:1] Likewise this is the law of the trespass offering: it is most holy. [2] In the place where they kill the burnt offering shall they kill the trespass offering: and the _____ thereof shall he sprinkle round about upon the _____. [3] And he shall offer of it all the fat thereof; the rump, and the fat that covereth the inwards, [4] And the two kidneys, and the fat that is on them, which is by the flanks, and the caul that is above the liver, with the kidneys, it shall he take away: [5] And the priest shall burn them upon the altar for an offering made by fire unto the Lord: it is a trespass offering. [6] Every male among the priests shall eat thereof: it shall be eaten in the holy place: it is most holy. [7] As the sin offering is, so is the trespass offering: there is one law for them: the priest that maketh _____ therewith shall have it. [8] And the priest that offereth any man's burnt offering, even the priest shall have to himself the skin of the burnt offering which he hath offered. [9] And all the meat offering that is baken in the oven, and all that is dressed in the fryingpan, and in the pan, shall be the priest's that offereth it. [10] And every meat offering, mingled with oil, and dry, shall all the sons of Aaron have, one as much as another. [11] And this is the law of the sacrifice of peace offerings, which he shall offer unto the Lord. [12] If he offer it for a thanksgiving, then he shall offer with the sacrifice of thanksgiving _____ cakes mingled with _____, and unleavened wafers anointed with oil, and cakes mingled with oil, of fine flour, fried. [13] Besides the cakes, he shall offer for his offering leavened bread with the sacrifice of _____ of his peace offerings. [14] And of it he shall offer one out of the whole oblation for an heave offering unto the Lord, and it shall be the priest's that sprinkleth the blood of the peace offerings. [15] And the flesh of the sacrifice of his peace offerings for _____ shall be eaten the same day that it is offered; he shall not leave any of it until the morning. [16] But if the sacrifice of his offering be a _____, or a voluntary offering, it shall be eaten the same day that he offereth his sacrifice: and on the morrow also the remainder of it shall be eaten: [17] But the remainder of the flesh of the sacrifice on the third day shall be burnt with fire. [18] And if any of the flesh of the sacrifice of his peace offerings be eaten at all on the third day, it shall not be accepted, neither shall it be imputed unto him that offereth it: it shall be an abomination, and the soul that eateth of it shall bear his iniquity. [19] And the flesh that toucheth any unclean thing shall not be eaten; it shall be burnt with fire: and as for the flesh, all that be clean shall eat thereof. [20] But the soul that eateth of the flesh of the sacrifice of peace offerings, that pertain unto the Lord, having his uncleanness upon him, even that soul shall be cut off from his people. [21] Moreover the soul that shall touch any unclean thing, as the uncleanness of man, or any unclean beast, or any abominable unclean thing, and eat of the flesh of the sacrifice of peace offerings, which pertain unto the Lord, even that soul shall be cut off from his people.

[22] And the Lord spake unto Moses, saying, [23] Speak unto the children of Israel, saying, Ye shall eat no manner of _____, of ox, or of sheep, or of goat. [24] And the fat of the beast that dieth of itself, and the fat of that which is torn with beasts, may be _____ in any other use: but ye shall in no wise _____ of it. [25] For whosoever eateth the fat of the beast, of which men offer an offering made by fire unto the Lord, even the soul that eateth it shall be cut off from his people. [26] Moreover ye

shall eat no manner of _____, whether it be of fowl or of beast, in any of your dwellings. [27] Whatsoever soul it be that eateth any manner of _____, even that soul shall be cut off from his people.

[28] And the Lord spake unto Moses, saying, [29] Speak unto the children of Israel, saying, He that offereth the sacrifice of his peace offerings unto the Lord shall bring his oblation unto the Lord of the sacrifice of his peace offerings. [30] His own hands shall bring the offerings of the Lord made by fire, the fat with the breast, it shall he bring, that the breast may be waved for a wave offering before the Lord. [31] And the priest shall burn the fat upon the altar: but the breast shall be Aaron's and his sons'. [32] And the right shoulder shall ye give unto the priest for an heave offering of the sacrifices of your peace offerings. [33] He among the sons of Aaron, that offereth the blood of the peace offerings, and the fat, shall have the right shoulder for his part. [34] For the wave breast and the heave shoulder have I taken of the children of Israel from off the sacrifices of their peace offerings, and have given them unto Aaron the priest and unto his sons by a statute for ever from among the children of Israel.

[35] This is the portion of the anointing of Aaron, and of the anointing of his sons, out of the offerings of the Lord made by fire, in the day when he presented them to _____ unto the Lord in the priest's _____; [36] Which the Lord commanded to be given them of the children of Israel, in the day that he anointed them, by a statute for ever throughout their generations. [37] This is the law of the burnt offering, of the meat offering, and of the sin offering, and of the trespass offering, and of the consecrations, and of the sacrifice of the peace offerings; [38] Which the Lord commanded Moses in mount _____, in the day that he commanded the children of Israel to offer their oblations unto the Lord, in the wilderness of Sinai.

[8:1] And the Lord spake unto Moses, saying, [2] Take Aaron and his sons with him, and the garments, and the anointing oil, and a bullock for the sin offering, and two rams, and a basket of unleavened bread; [3] And gather thou all the congregation together unto the door of the tabernacle of the congregation. [4] And Moses did as the Lord commanded him; and the assembly was gathered together unto the door of the tabernacle of the congregation. [5] And Moses said unto the congregation, This is the thing which the Lord commanded to be done. [6] And Moses brought Aaron and his sons, and washed them with water. [7] And he put upon him the coat, and girded him with the girdle, and clothed him with the robe, and put the ephod upon him, and he girded him with the curious girdle of the ephod, and bound it unto him therewith. [8] And he put the breastplate upon him: also he put in the breastplate the _____ and the _____. [9] And he put the mitre upon his head; also upon the mitre, even upon his forefront, did he put the golden plate, the holy crown; as the Lord commanded Moses. [10] And Moses took the anointing _____, and anointed the tabernacle and all that was therein, and sanctified them. [11] And he sprinkled thereof upon the altar _____ times, and anointed the altar and all his vessels, both the laver and his foot, to _____ them. [12] And he poured of the anointing oil upon Aaron's _____, and anointed him, to _____ him. [13] And Moses brought Aaron's sons, and put coats upon them, and girded them with girdles, and put bonnets upon them; as the Lord commanded Moses. [14] And he brought the bullock for the sin offering: and Aaron and his sons laid their hands upon the head of the bullock for the sin offering. [15] And he slew it; and Moses took the blood, and put it upon the horns of the altar round about with his finger, and _____the altar, and poured the blood at the bottom of the altar, and _____it, to make _____upon it. [16] And he took all the fat that was upon the inwards, and caul above the liver, and the two kidneys, and their fat, and Moses burned it upon the altar. [17] But the bullock, and his hide, his flesh, and his dung, he burnt with fire without the camp; as the Lord commanded Moses.

[18] And he brought the ram for the burnt offering: and Aaron and his sons laid their hands upon the head of the ram. [19] And he killed it; and Moses sprinkled the _____upon the _____round about. [20] And he cut the ram into pieces; and Moses burnt the head, and the pieces, and the fat. [21] And he washed the inwards and the legs in water; and Moses burnt the whole ram upon the altar: it was a burnt sacrifice for a sweet savour, and an offering made by fire unto the Lord; as the Lord commanded Moses.

[22] And he brought the other ram, the ram of _____: and Aaron and his sons laid their hands upon the head of the ram. [23] And he slew it; and Moses took of the blood of it, and put it upon the tip of Aaron's right _____, and upon the _____of his right hand, and upon the great _____of his right foot. [24] And he brought Aaron's sons, and Moses put of the blood upon the tip of their right _____, and upon the _____of their right hands, and upon the great _____of their right feet: and Moses sprinkled the blood upon the altar round about. [25] And he took the fat, and the rump, and all the fat that was upon the inwards, and the caul above the liver, and the two kidneys, and their fat, and the right shoulder: [26] And out of the basket of _____bread, that was before the Lord, he took one unleavened cake, and a cake of oiled bread, and one wafer, and put them on the fat, and upon the right _____: [27] And he put all upon Aaron's hands, and upon his sons' hands, and _____them for a wave offering before the Lord. [28] And Moses took them from off their hands, and burnt them on the altar upon the burnt offering: they were consecrations for a sweet savour: it is an offering made by fire unto the Lord. [29] And Moses took the breast, and waved it for a wave offering before the Lord: for of the ram of consecration it was Moses' part; as the Lord commanded Moses. [30] And Moses took of the anointing _____, and of the _____which was upon the _____, and sprinkled it upon _____, and upon his _____, and upon his _____, and upon his sons' _____with him; and _____ _____, and his _____, and his _____, and his sons' _____with him.

[31] And Moses said unto Aaron and to his sons, _____the flesh at the door of the tabernacle of the congregation: and there _____it with the bread that is in the basket of consecrations, as I commanded, saying, Aaron and his sons shall eat it. [32] And that which remaineth of the flesh and of the bread shall ye burn with fire. [33] And ye shall not go out of the door of the tabernacle of the congregation in _____days, until the days of your _____be at an end: for _____days shall he consecrate you. [34] As he hath done this day, so the Lord hath commanded to do, to make an atonement for you. [35] Therefore shall ye abide at the door of the tabernacle of the congregation day and night seven days, and keep the charge of the Lord, that ye _____not: for so I am commanded. [36] So Aaron and his sons did all things which the Lord commanded by the hand of Moses.

[9:1] And it came to pass on the _____ day, that Moses called Aaron and his sons, and the _____ of Israel; [2] And he said unto Aaron, Take thee a young calf for a sin offering, and a ram for a burnt offering, without _____, and offer them before the Lord. [3] And unto the children of Israel thou shalt speak, saying, Take ye a kid of the goats for a sin offering; and a calf and a lamb, both of the _____ year, without blemish, for a burnt offering; [4] Also a bullock and a ram for peace offerings, to sacrifice before the Lord; and a meat offering mingled with _____: for to day the Lord will appear unto you.

[5] And they brought that which Moses commanded before the tabernacle of the congregation: and all the congregation drew near and stood before the Lord. [6] And Moses said, This is the thing which the Lord commanded that ye should do: and the _____ of the Lord shall appear unto you. [7] And Moses said unto Aaron, Go unto the altar, and offer thy sin offering, and thy burnt offering, and make an atonement for thyself, and for the people: and offer the offering of the people, and make an _____ for them; as the Lord commanded.

[8] Aaron therefore went unto the altar, and slew the calf of the sin offering, which was for himself. [9] And the sons of Aaron brought the blood unto him: and he dipped his finger in the blood, and put it upon the horns of the altar, and poured out the blood at the bottom of the altar: [10] But the fat, and the kidneys, and the caul above the liver of the sin offering, he burnt upon the altar; as the Lord commanded Moses. [11] And the flesh and the hide he burnt with fire without the camp. [12] And he slew the burnt offering; and Aaron's sons presented unto him the blood, which he sprinkled round about upon the altar. [13] And they presented the burnt offering unto him, with the pieces thereof, and the head: and he burnt them upon the altar. [14] And he did wash the inwards and the legs, and burnt them upon the burnt offering on the altar.

[15] And he brought the people's offering, and took the goat, which was the sin offering for the people, and slew it, and offered it for sin, as the first. [16] And he brought the burnt offering, and offered it according to the manner. [17] And he brought the meat offering, and took an handful thereof, and burnt it upon the altar, beside the burnt sacrifice of the morning. [18] He slew also the bullock and the ram for a sacrifice of peace offerings, which was for the people: and Aaron's sons presented unto him the blood, which he sprinkled upon the altar round about, [19] And the fat of the bullock and of the ram, the rump, and that which covereth the inwards, and the kidneys, and the caul above the liver: [20] And they put the fat upon the breasts, and he burnt the fat upon the altar: [21] And the breasts and the right shoulder Aaron waved for a wave offering before the Lord; as Moses commanded. [22] And Aaron lifted up his hand toward the people, and _____ them, and came down from offering of the sin offering, and the burnt offering, and peace offerings. [23] And Moses and Aaron went into the tabernacle of the congregation, and came out, and _____ the people: and the _____ of the Lord appeared unto all the people. [24] And there came a fire out from before the Lord, and consumed upon the altar the burnt offering and the fat: which when all the people saw, they _____, and fell on their faces.

[10:1] And _____ and _____, the sons of Aaron, took either of them _____ censer, and put fire therein, and put incense thereon, and offered _____ fire before the Lord, which he commanded them _____. [2] And there went out _____ from the Lord, and _____ them, and they

_____ before the Lord. [3] Then Moses said unto Aaron, This is it that the Lord spake, saying, I will be _____ in them that come _____ me, and before all the _____ I will be glorified. And Aaron held his _____. [4] And Moses called Mishael and Elzaphan, the sons of Uzziel the uncle of Aaron, and said unto them, Come near, carry your brethren from before the sanctuary out of the camp. [5] So they went near, and carried them in their coats out of the camp; as Moses had said. [6] And Moses said unto Aaron, and unto Eleazar and unto Ithamar, his sons, Uncover not your heads, neither _____ your clothes; lest ye _____, and lest wrath come upon all the people: but let your brethren, the whole house of Israel, _____ the _____ which the Lord hath kindled. [7] And ye shall not go out from the door of the tabernacle of the congregation, lest ye die: for the anointing _____ of the Lord is upon you. And they did according to the word of Moses.

[8] And the Lord spake unto _____, saying, [9] Do _____ drink _____ nor strong _____, thou, nor thy _____ with thee, when ye go into the tabernacle of the congregation, lest ye _____: it shall be a statute for ever throughout your generations: [10] And that ye may put _____ between _____ and _____, and between _____ and _____; [11] And that ye may _____ the children of Israel _____ the _____ which the Lord hath spoken unto them by the hand of Moses.

[12] And Moses spake unto _____, and unto _____ and unto _____, his sons that were left, Take the meat offering that remaineth of the offerings of the Lord made by fire, and eat it without leaven beside the altar: for it is most holy: [13] And ye shall eat it in the holy place, because it is thy _____, and thy sons' due, of the sacrifices of the Lord made by fire: for so I am commanded. [14] And the wave breast and heave shoulder shall ye eat in a clean place; thou, and thy sons, and thy daughters with thee: for they be thy _____, and thy sons' due, which are _____ out of the _____ of peace offerings of the children of Israel. [15] The heave shoulder and the wave breast shall they bring with the offerings made by fire of the fat, to wave it for a wave offering before the Lord; and it shall be _____, and thy sons' with thee, by a statute for ever; as the Lord hath commanded.

[16] And Moses diligently sought the goat of the sin offering, and, behold, it was burnt: and he was _____ with Eleazar and Ithamar, the sons of Aaron which were left alive, saying, [17] Wherefore have ye not _____ the sin offering in the holy place, seeing it is most holy, and God hath given it you to _____ the _____ of the congregation, to make _____ for them before the Lord? [18] Behold, the blood of it was not brought in within the holy place: ye should indeed have eaten it in the holy place, as I commanded. [19] And Aaron said unto Moses, Behold, this day have they offered their sin offering and their burnt offering before the Lord; and such things have befallen me: and if I had eaten the sin offering to day, should it have been accepted in the sight of the Lord? [20] And when Moses heard that, he was content.

[11:1] And the Lord spake unto Moses and to Aaron, saying unto them, [2] Speak unto the children of Israel, saying, These are the _____ which ye shall _____ among all the beasts that are on the earth. [3] Whatsoever _____ the _____, and is _____, _____ cheweth the _____, among the beasts, that _____ ye _____. [4] Nevertheless these shall ye _____ eat of them that chew the cud, _____ of them that divide the hoof: as the camel, because he cheweth the cud, _____ divideth _____ the hoof; he is _____ unto you. [5] And the coney, because he cheweth the cud, _____ divideth _____ the hoof; he is _____ unto you. [6] And the hare, because he cheweth the cud, _____ divideth _____ the hoof; he is unclean unto you. [7] And the swine, though he divide the hoof, and be clovenfooted, yet he cheweth _____ the cud; he is _____ to you. [8] Of their flesh shall ye _____ eat, and their carcase shall ye not touch; they are _____ to you.

[9] These _____ ye _____ of all that are in the _____ : whatsoever _____ _____ and _____ in the _____ , in the _____ , and in the rivers, them shall ye eat. [10] And all that have _____ fins and scales in the seas, and in the rivers, of all that move in the waters, and of any living thing which is in the waters, they shall be an _____ unto you: [11] They shall be even an abomination unto you; ye shall not eat of their flesh, but ye shall have their carcases in abomination. [12] Whatsoever hath _____ fins _____ scales in the waters, that shall be an _____ unto you.

[13] And these are they which ye shall have in _____ among the _____ ; they shall _____ be _____ , they are an abomination: the _____ , and the _____ , and the _____ , [14] And the _____ , and the _____ after his kind; [15] Every _____ after his kind; [16] And the _____ , and the _____ _____ , and the _____ , and the _____ after his kind, [17] And the little _____ , and the _____ , and the great _____ , [18] And the _____ , and the _____ , and the gier _____ , [19] And the _____ , the _____ after her kind, and the _____ , and the _____ . [20] _____ fowls that _____ , going upon all _____ , shall be an _____ unto you. [21] Yet _____ may ye _____ of every _____ creeping thing that goeth upon all _____ , which have _____ above their _____ , to _____ withal upon the earth; [22] Even these of them ye may eat; the _____ after his kind, and the _____ locust after his kind, and the _____ after his kind, and the _____ after his kind. [23] But all other flying creeping things, which have _____ feet, shall be an abomination unto you. [24] And for these ye shall be unclean: whosoever toucheth the carcase of them shall be unclean until the _____ . [25] And whosoever beareth ought of the carcase of them shall wash his clothes, and be unclean until the even. [26] The carcases of every beast which divideth the _____ , and is not _____ , nor cheweth the _____ , are unclean unto you: every one that toucheth them shall be unclean. [27] And whatsoever goeth upon his _____ , among all manner of beasts that go on all _____ , those are unclean unto you: whoso toucheth their carcase shall be unclean until the even. [28] And he that beareth the carcase of them shall wash his clothes, and be unclean until the even: they are unclean unto you.

[29] These also shall be unclean unto you among the creeping things that creep upon the earth; the _____ , and the _____ , and the _____ after his kind, [30] And the _____ , and the _____ , and the _____ , and the _____ , and the _____ . [31] These are unclean to you among all that creep: whosoever doth touch them, when they be _____ , shall be unclean until the even. [32] And upon whatsoever any of them, when they are dead, doth _____ , it shall

be unclean; whether it be any vessel of wood, or raiment, or skin, or sack, whatsoever vessel it be, wherein any work is done, it must be put into _____, and it shall be unclean until the even; so it shall be cleansed. [33] And every earthen vessel, whereinto any of them falleth, whatsoever is in it shall be unclean; and ye shall _____ it. [34] Of all _____ which may be _____, that on which such _____ cometh shall be unclean: and all _____ that may be drunk in every such vessel shall be unclean. [35] And every thing whereupon any part of their carcase falleth shall be unclean; whether it be _____, or _____ for _____, they shall be _____ down: for they are unclean, and shall be unclean unto you. [36] Nevertheless a _____ or _____, wherein there is _____ of water, shall be clean: but that which toucheth their carcase shall be unclean. [37] And if any part of their carcase fall upon any sowing _____ which is to be sown, it shall be clean. [38] But if any water be put upon the seed, and any part of their carcase fall thereon, it shall be unclean unto you. [39] And if any beast, of which ye may eat, die; he that toucheth the carcase thereof shall be unclean until the even. [40] And he that eateth of the carcase of it shall wash his clothes, and be unclean until the even: he also that beareth the carcase of it shall wash his clothes, and be unclean until the even. [41] And every _____ thing that creepeth upon the earth shall be an _____; it shall not be eaten. [42] Whatsoever goeth upon the _____, and whatsoever goeth upon all _____, or whatsoever hath _____ _____ among all creeping things that creep upon the earth, them ye shall _____ eat; for they are an abomination. [43] Ye shall not make yourselves abominable with any creeping thing that creepeth, neither shall ye make yourselves unclean with them, that ye should be _____ thereby. [44] For I am the Lord your God: ye shall therefore _____ yourselves, and ye shall be _____; for I am _____: neither shall ye _____ yourselves with any manner of creeping thing that creepeth upon the earth. [45] For I am the Lord that _____ you _____ out of the land of Egypt, to be your _____: ye shall therefore be _____, for I am _____. [46] This is the law of the beasts, and of the fowl, and of every living creature that moveth in the waters, and of every creature that creepeth upon the earth: [47] To make a _____ between the _____ and the _____, and between the beast that may be _____ and the beast that may _____ be eaten.

[12:1] And the Lord spake unto Moses, saying, [2] Speak unto the children of Israel, saying, If a woman have conceived seed, and born a _____ child: then she shall be unclean _____ days; according to the days of the separation for her infirmity shall she be unclean. [3] And in the _____ day the flesh of his foreskin shall be _____. [4] And she shall then continue in the _____ of her purifying three and thirty days; she shall touch no hallowed thing, nor come into the sanctuary, until the days of her purifying be fulfilled. [5] But if she bear a _____ child, then she shall be unclean _____ weeks, as in her separation: and she shall continue in the blood of her purifying threescore and six days. [6] And when the days of her purifying are fulfilled, for a son, or for a daughter, she shall bring a lamb of the first year for a burnt offering, and a young pigeon, or a turtledove, for a sin offering, unto the door of the tabernacle of the congregation, unto the priest: [7] Who shall offer it before the Lord, and make an _____ for her; and she shall be cleansed from the _____ of her blood. This is the law for her that hath born a male or a female. [8] And if she be not able to bring a lamb, then she shall bring two turtles, or two young pigeons; the one for the burnt offering, and the other for a sin offering: and the priest shall make an atonement for her, and she shall be clean.

[13:1] And the Lord spake unto Moses and Aaron, saying, [2] When a man shall have in the skin of his flesh a rising, a scab, or a bright spot, and it be in the skin of his flesh like the plague of _____; then he shall be brought unto Aaron the priest, or unto one of his sons the priests: [3] And the _____ shall look on the plague in the skin of the flesh: and when the hair in the plague is turned _____ , and the plague in sight be deeper than the skin of his flesh, it is a plague of leprosy: and the priest shall look on him, and pronounce him _____. [4] If the bright spot be white in the skin of his flesh, and in sight be not deeper than the skin, and the hair thereof be not turned white; then the priest shall shut up him that hath the plague _____days: [5] And the priest shall look on him the seventh day: and, behold, if the plague in his sight be at a stay, and the plague spread not in the skin; then the priest shall shut him up seven days more: [6] And the priest shall look on him again the seventh day: and, behold, if the plague be somewhat dark, and the plague spread not in the skin, the priest shall pronounce him clean: it is but a scab: and he shall wash his clothes, and be clean. [7] But if the scab spread much abroad in the skin, after that he hath been seen of the priest for his cleansing, he shall be seen of the priest again: [8] And if the priest see that, behold, the scab spreadeth in the skin, then the priest shall pronounce him unclean: it is a leprosy.

[9] When the plague of leprosy is in a man, then he shall be brought unto the priest; [10] And the priest shall see him: and, behold, if the rising be white in the skin, and it have turned the hair white, and there be quick raw flesh in the rising; [11] It is an old leprosy in the skin of his flesh, and the priest shall pronounce him unclean, and shall not shut him up: for he is unclean. [12] And if a leprosy break out abroad in the skin, and the leprosy cover all the skin of him that hath the plague from his head even to his foot, wheresoever the priest looketh; [13] Then the priest shall _____: and, behold, if the leprosy have covered all his flesh, he shall pronounce him clean that hath the plague: it is all turned white: he is _____. [14] But when raw flesh appeareth in him, he shall be unclean. [15] And the priest shall see the raw flesh, and pronounce him to be unclean: for the raw flesh is unclean: it is a leprosy. [16] Or if the raw flesh turn again, and be changed unto white, he shall come unto the priest; [17] And the priest shall see him: and, behold, if the plague be turned into white; then the priest shall pronounce him clean that hath the plague: he is clean.

[18] The flesh also, in which, even in the skin thereof, was a boil, and is healed, [19] And in the place of the boil there be a white rising, or a bright spot, white, and somewhat reddish, and it be shewed to the priest; [20] And if, when the priest seeth it, behold, it be in sight lower than the skin, and the hair thereof be turned white; the priest shall pronounce him unclean: it is a plague of leprosy broken out of the boil. [21] But if the priest look on it, and, behold, there be no white hairs therein, and if it be not lower than the skin, but be somewhat dark; then the priest shall shut him up seven days: [22] And if it spread much abroad in the skin, then the priest shall pronounce him unclean: it is a plague. [23] But if the bright spot stay in his place, and spread not, it is a burning _____; and the priest shall pronounce him clean.

LEVITICUS

[24] Or if there be any flesh, in the skin whereof there is a hot burning, and the quick flesh that burneth have a white bright spot, somewhat reddish, or white; [25] Then the priest shall look upon it: and, behold, if the hair in the bright spot be turned white, and it be in sight deeper than the skin; it is a leprosy broken out of the burning: wherefore the priest shall pronounce him unclean: it is the plague of leprosy. [26] But if the priest look on it, and, behold, there be no white hair in the bright spot, and it be no lower than the other skin, but be somewhat dark; then the priest shall shut him up seven days: [27] And the priest shall look upon him the seventh day: and if it be spread much abroad in the skin, then the priest shall pronounce him unclean: it is the plague of leprosy. [28] And if the bright spot stay in his place, and spread not in the skin, but it be somewhat dark; it is a rising of the burning, and the priest shall pronounce him clean: for it is an inflammation of the burning.

[29] If a man or woman have a plague upon the _____ or the _____; [30] Then the priest shall see the plague: and, behold, if it be in sight deeper than the skin; and there be in it a _____ thin hair; then the priest shall pronounce him unclean: it is a dry _____, even a _____ upon the head or beard. [31] And if the priest look on the plague of the scall, and, behold, it be not in sight deeper than the skin, and that there is no black hair in it; then the priest shall shut up him that hath the plague of the scall seven days: [32] And in the seventh day the priest shall look on the plague: and, behold, if the scall spread not, and there be in it no yellow hair, and the scall be not in sight deeper than the skin; [33] He shall be _____, but the scall shall he _____ shave; and the priest shall shut up him that hath the scall seven days more: [34] And in the seventh day the priest shall look on the scall: and, behold, if the scall be not spread in the skin, nor be in sight deeper than the skin; then the priest shall pronounce him clean: and he shall wash his clothes, and be clean. [35] But if the scall spread much in the skin after his cleansing; [36] Then the priest shall look on him: and, behold, if the scall be spread in the skin, the priest shall not seek for yellow hair; he is unclean. [37] But if the scall be in his sight at a stay, and that there is _____ hair grown up therein; the scall is healed, he is clean: and the priest shall pronounce him clean.

[38] If a man also or a woman have in the skin of their flesh bright spots, even white bright spots; [39] Then the priest shall look: and, behold, if the bright spots in the skin of their flesh be darkish white; it is a _____ spot that groweth in the skin; he is clean. [40] And the man whose _____ is fallen _____ his head, he is _____; yet is he _____. [41] And he that hath his hair fallen off from the part of his head toward his face, he is _____ bald: yet is he _____. [42] And if there be in the bald head, or bald forehead, a white reddish sore; it is a leprosy sprung up in his bald head, or his bald forehead. [43] Then the priest shall look upon it: and, behold, if the rising of the sore be white reddish in his bald head, or in his bald forehead, as the leprosy appeareth in the skin of the flesh; [44] He is a leprous man, he is unclean: the priest shall pronounce him utterly unclean; his plague is in his _____. [45] And the leper in whom the plague is, his clothes shall be _____, and his head _____, and he shall put a covering upon his upper _____, and shall cry, _____, _____. [46] All the days wherein the plague shall be in him he shall be _____; he is unclean: he shall dwell _____; without the camp shall his habitation be.

16

[47] The garment also that the plague of leprosy is in, whether it be a woollen garment, or a linen garment; [48] Whether it be in the warp, or woof; of linen, or of woollen; whether in a skin, or in any thing made of skin; [49] And if the plague be _____ or _____ in the garment, or in the skin, either in the warp, or in the woof, or in any thing of skin; it is a plague of leprosy, and shall be shewed unto the priest: [50] And the priest shall look upon the plague, and shut up it that hath the plague seven days: [51] And he shall look on the plague on the seventh day: if the plague be spread in the garment, either in the warp, or in the woof, or in a skin, or in any work that is made of skin; the plague is a fretting leprosy; it is unclean. [52] He shall therefore _____ that garment, whether warp or woof, in woollen or in linen, or any thing of skin, wherein the plague is: for it is a fretting leprosy; it shall be burnt in the fire. [53] And if the priest shall look, and, behold, the plague be not spread in the garment, either in the warp, or in the woof, or in any thing of skin; [54] Then the priest shall command that they wash the thing wherein the plague is, and he shall shut it up seven days more: [55] And the priest shall look on the plague, after that it is washed: and, behold, if the plague have not changed his colour, and the plague be not spread; it is unclean; thou shalt burn it in the fire; it is fret inward, whether it be bare within or without. [56] And if the priest look, and, behold, the plague be somewhat dark after the washing of it; then he shall rend it out of the garment, or out of the skin, or out of the warp, or out of the woof: [57] And if it appear still in the garment, either in the warp, or in the woof, or in any thing of skin; it is a spreading plague: thou shalt burn that wherein the plague is with fire. [58] And the garment, either warp, or woof, or whatsoever thing of skin it be, which thou shalt wash, if the plague be departed from them, then it shall be washed the second time, and shall be clean. [59] This is the law of the plague of leprosy in a garment of woollen or linen, either in the warp, or woof, or any thing of skins, to pronounce it clean, or to pronounce it unclean.

[14:1] And the Lord spake unto Moses, saying, [2] This shall be the law of the _____ in the _____ of his _____: He shall be brought unto the _____: [3] And the _____ shall go forth _____ of the _____; and the priest shall _____, and, behold, if the plague of leprosy be healed in the leper; [4] Then shall the priest _____ to take for him that is to be cleansed two birds alive and clean, and cedar wood, and scarlet, and hyssop: [5] And the priest shall command that one of the birds be _____ in an earthen vessel over running water: [6] As for the living bird, he shall take it, and the cedar wood, and the scarlet, and the hyssop, and shall dip them and the living bird in the blood of the bird that was killed over the running water: [7] And he shall sprinkle upon him that is to be cleansed from the leprosy seven times, and shall pronounce him clean, and shall let the living bird loose into the open field. [8] And he that is to be cleansed shall wash his clothes, and _____ off all his hair, and wash himself in water, that he may be clean: and after that he shall come into the camp, and shall tarry abroad out of his tent seven days. [9] But it shall be on the seventh day, that he shall shave all his hair off his _____ and his _____ and his _____, even all his hair he shall shave off: and he shall wash his clothes, also he shall wash his flesh in water, and he shall be clean. [10] And on the eighth day he shall take two he lambs without blemish, and one ewe lamb of the first year without blemish, and three tenth deals of fine flour for a meat offering, mingled with oil, and one log of oil. [11] And the priest that maketh him clean shall present the man that is to be made clean, and those things, before the Lord, at the door of the tabernacle of the congregation: [12] And the priest shall take one he lamb, and offer him for a trespass offering, and the log of oil, and wave them for a wave offering before the Lord: [13] And he shall slay the lamb in the place where he shall kill the sin offering and the burnt offering, in the holy place: for as the sin offering is the priest's, so is the trespass offering: it is most holy: [14] And the priest shall take some of the blood of the trespass offering, and the priest shall put it upon the tip of the right ear of him that is to be cleansed, and upon the thumb of his right hand, and upon the great toe of his right foot: [15] And the priest shall take some of the log of oil, and pour it into the _____ of his own _____ hand: [16] And the priest shall dip his _____ finger in the oil that is in his _____ hand, and shall sprinkle of the _____ with his finger _____ times before the Lord: [17] And of the rest of the oil that is in his hand shall the priest put upon the tip of the right ear of him that is to be cleansed, and upon the thumb of his right hand, and upon the great toe of his right foot, upon the blood of the trespass offering: [18] And the remnant of the oil that is in the priest's hand he shall pour upon the _____ of him that is to be cleansed: and the priest shall make an atonement for him before the Lord. [19] And the priest shall offer the sin offering, and make an atonement for him that is to be cleansed from his uncleanness; and afterward he shall kill the burnt offering: [20] And the priest shall offer the burnt offering and the meat offering upon the _____ : and the priest shall make an atonement for him, and he shall be clean. [21] And if he be _____ , and cannot get so much; then he shall take one lamb for a trespass offering to be waved, to make an atonement for him, and one tenth deal of fine flour mingled with oil for a meat offering, and a log of oil; [22] And two turtledoves, or two young pigeons, such as he is _____ to get; and the one shall be a sin offering, and the other a burnt offering. [23] And he shall bring them on the eighth day for his cleansing unto the priest, unto the door of the tabernacle of the congregation, before the Lord. [24] And the priest shall take the lamb of the trespass offering, and the log of oil, and the priest shall wave them for a wave offering before the Lord: [25] And he shall kill the lamb of the trespass offering, and the priest shall take some of the blood of the trespass offering, and put it upon the tip of the right ear of him that is to be cleansed, and upon the thumb of his right hand, and upon the great toe of his right foot: [26] And the priest shall pour of the oil into the palm of his own left hand: [27] And the priest shall sprinkle with his right finger some of the oil that is in his left hand seven times before the Lord: [28] And the priest shall put of the oil that is in his hand upon the _____ of the right _____ of him that is to be cleansed, and upon the _____ of his right _____ , and upon the _____ toe of his _____ foot, _____ the place of the _____ of the trespass offering: [29] And the rest of the oil that is in the priest's hand he shall put upon the head of him that is to be cleansed, to make an _____ for him before the Lord. [30] And he shall offer the one of the turtledoves, or of the young pigeons, such as he can get; [31] Even such as he is _____ to get, the one for a sin offering, and the other for a burnt offering, with the meat offering: and the priest shall make an atonement for him that is to be cleansed before the Lord. [32] This is the law of him in whom is the plague of leprosy, whose hand is not able to get that which pertaineth to his cleansing.

[33] And the Lord spake unto Moses and unto Aaron, saying, [34] When ye be come into the land of _____ , which _____ give to you for a _____ , and I

LEVITICUS

_____ the plague of _____ in a house of the land of your possession; [35] And he that _____ the house shall come and tell the priest, saying, It seemeth to me there is as it were a plague in the house: [36] Then the priest shall command that they _____ the house, before the priest go into it to see the plague, that all that is in the house be not made unclean: and afterward the priest shall go in to see the house: [37] And he shall look on the plague, and, behold, if the plague be in the walls of the house with hollow strakes, _____ or _____, which in sight are lower than the wall; [38] Then the priest shall go out of the house to the door of the house, and shut up the house seven days: [39] And the priest shall come again the seventh day, and shall look: and, behold, if the plague be spread in the walls of the house; [40] Then the priest shall command that they take away the stones in which the plague is, and they shall cast them into an unclean place _____ the city: [41] And he shall cause the house to be scraped within round about, and they shall pour out the dust that they scrape off without the city into an unclean place: [42] And they shall take other stones, and put them in the place of those stones; and he shall take other morter, and shall plaister the house. [43] And if the plague come again, and break out in the house, after that he hath taken away the stones, and after he hath scraped the house, and after it is plaistered; [44] Then the priest shall come and look, and, behold, if the plague be spread in the house, it is a fretting leprosy in the house: it is unclean. [45] And he shall break down the house, the stones of it, and the timber thereof, and all the morter of the house; and he shall carry them forth out of the city into an unclean place. [46] Moreover he that goeth into the house all the while that it is shut up shall be unclean until the even. [47] And he that lieth in the house shall wash his clothes; and he that eateth in the house shall wash his clothes. [48] And if the _____ shall _____ in, and _____ upon it, and, behold, the plague hath not spread in the house, after the house was plaistered: then the priest shall pronounce the house clean, because the plague is healed. [49] And he shall take to cleanse the house two birds, and cedar wood, and scarlet, and hyssop: [50] And he shall kill the one of the birds in an earthen vessel over running water: [51] And he shall take the cedar wood, and the hyssop, and the scarlet, and the living bird, and dip them in the blood of the slain bird, and in the running water, and sprinkle the house _____ times: [52] And he shall cleanse the house with the blood of the bird, and with the running water, and with the living bird, and with the cedar wood, and with the hyssop, and with the scarlet: [53] But he shall let go the living bird out of the city into the open fields, and make an atonement for the house: and it shall be clean. [54] This is the law for all manner of plague of leprosy, and scall, [55] And for the leprosy of a garment, and of a house, [56] And for a rising, and for a scab, and for a bright spot: [57] To _____ when it is _____, and when it is _____: this is the law of leprosy.

[15:1] And the Lord spake unto Moses and to Aaron, saying, [2] Speak unto the children of Israel, and say unto them, When any man hath a running issue out of his flesh, because of his issue he is unclean. [3] And this shall be his uncleanness in his issue: whether his flesh run with his issue, or his flesh be stopped from his issue, it is his uncleanness. [4] Every _____, whereon he lieth that hath the issue, is unclean: and every thing, whereon he _____, shall be unclean. [5] And whosoever _____ his bed shall wash his clothes, and bathe himself in water, and be unclean until the even. [6] And he that sitteth on any thing whereon he sat that hath the issue shall wash his clothes, and bathe himself in water, and be unclean until the even. [7] And he that toucheth the flesh of him that hath the issue shall wash his clothes, and bathe himself in water, and be unclean until the even. [8] And if he that hath the issue _____ upon him that is clean; then he shall wash his clothes, and bathe himself in water, and be unclean until the even. [9] And what _____ soever he rideth upon that hath the issue shall be unclean. [10] And whosoever toucheth any thing that was under him shall be unclean until the even: and he that beareth any of those things shall wash his clothes, and bathe himself in water, and be unclean until the even. [11] And whomsoever he toucheth that hath the issue, and hath not rinsed his hands in water, he shall wash his clothes, and bathe himself in water, and be unclean until the even. [12] And the vessel of earth, that he toucheth which hath the issue, shall be _____ : and every vessel of _____ shall be _____ in water. [13] And when he that hath an issue is cleansed of his issue; then he shall number to himself seven days for his cleansing, and wash his clothes, and bathe his flesh in running water, and shall be clean. [14] And on the eighth day he shall take to him two turtledoves, or two young pigeons, and come before the Lord unto the door of the tabernacle of the congregation, and give them unto the priest: [15] And the priest shall offer them, the one for a sin offering, and the other for a burnt offering; and the priest shall make an atonement for him before the Lord for his issue. [16] And if any man's seed of copulation go out from him, then he shall wash all his flesh in water, and be unclean until the even. [17] And every garment, and every skin, whereon is the seed of copulation, shall be washed with water, and be unclean until the even. [18] The woman also with whom man shall lie with seed of copulation, they shall both bathe themselves in water, and be unclean until the even.

[19] And if a woman have an issue, and her issue in her flesh be blood, she shall be put apart seven days: and whosoever toucheth her shall be unclean until the even. [20] And every thing that she lieth upon in her separation shall be unclean: every thing also that she sitteth upon shall be unclean. [21] And whosoever toucheth her bed shall wash his clothes, and bathe himself in water, and be unclean until the even. [22] And whosoever toucheth any thing that she sat upon shall wash his clothes, and bathe himself in water, and be unclean until the even. [23] And if it be on her bed, or on any thing whereon she sitteth, when he toucheth it, he shall be unclean until the even. [24] And if any man lie with her at all, and her flowers be upon him, he shall be unclean seven days; and all the bed whereon he lieth shall be unclean. [25] And if a woman have an issue of her blood many days out of the time of her separation, or if it run beyond the time of her separation; all the days of the issue of her uncleanness shall be as the days of her separation: she shall be unclean. [26] Every bed whereon she lieth all the days of her issue shall be unto her as the bed of her separation: and whatsoever she sitteth upon shall be unclean, as the uncleanness of her separation. [27] And whosoever toucheth those things shall be unclean, and shall wash his clothes, and bathe himself in water, and be unclean until the even. [28] But if she be _____ of her issue, then she shall number to herself seven days, and after that she shall be clean. [29] And on the eighth day she shall take unto her two turtles, or two young pigeons, and bring them unto the priest, to the door of the tabernacle of the congregation. [30] And the priest shall offer the one for a sin offering, and the other for a burnt offering; and the priest shall make an atonement for her before the Lord for the issue of her uncleanness. [31] Thus shall ye _____ the children of Israel from their uncleanness; that they die not in their uncleanness, when they

_____my _____that is among them. [32] This is the law of him that hath an issue, and of him whose seed goeth from him, and is defiled therewith; [33] And of her that is sick of her flowers, and of him that hath an issue, of the man, and of the woman, and of him that lieth with her that is unclean.

[16:1] And the Lord spake unto Moses after the _____of the _____sons of _____, when they offered before the Lord, and _____; [2] And the Lord said unto Moses, Speak unto Aaron thy brother, that he come not at all times into the _____place _____the _____before the _____seat, which is upon the _____; that he die _____: for I will appear in the _____upon the _____seat. [3] Thus shall Aaron come into the holy place: with a young bullock for a sin offering, and a ram for a burnt offering. [4] He shall put on the _____linen coat, and he shall have the linen _____upon his flesh, and shall be girded with a linen girdle, and with the linen mitre shall he be attired: these are holy _____; therefore shall he _____his flesh in water, and so put them on. [5] And he shall take of the congregation of the children of Israel two kids of the goats for a sin offering, and one ram for a burnt offering. [6] And Aaron shall offer his bullock of the sin offering, which is for _____, and make an _____for himself, and for his _____. [7] And he shall take the two goats, and present them before the Lord at the door of the tabernacle of the congregation. [8] And Aaron shall cast lots upon the two goats; one lot for the _____, and the other lot for the _____. [9] And Aaron shall bring the goat upon which the Lord's lot fell, and offer him for a sin offering. [10] But the goat, on which the lot fell to be the scapegoat, shall be presented _____before the Lord, to make an _____with him, and to let him _____for a scapegoat into the _____. [11] And Aaron shall bring the bullock of the sin offering, which is for himself, and shall make an atonement for himself, and for his house, and shall kill the bullock of the sin offering which is for himself: [12] And he shall take a censer full of burning coals of _____from off the _____before the Lord, and his _____full of sweet _____beaten small, and bring it _____the vail: [13] And he shall put the incense upon the fire before the Lord, that the cloud of the incense may cover the mercy seat that is upon the testimony, that he die not: [14] And he shall take of the blood of the bullock, and sprinkle it with his finger upon the mercy seat eastward; and before the mercy seat shall he sprinkle of the _____with his finger ___ _____times.

[15] Then shall he kill the goat of the sin offering, that is for the people, and bring his blood within the vail, and do with that blood as he did with the blood of the bullock, and sprinkle it upon the mercy seat, and before the mercy seat: [16] And he shall make an atonement for the holy place, because of the _____of the children of Israel, and because of their _____in all their _____: and so shall he do for the tabernacle of the congregation, that remaineth among them in the midst of their uncleanness. [17] And there shall be no man in the tabernacle of the congregation when he goeth in to make an atonement in the holy place, until he come out, and have made an atonement for himself, and for his household, and for all the congregation of Israel. [18] And he shall go out unto the altar that is before the Lord, and make an atonement for it; and shall take of the blood of the bullock, and of the blood of the goat, and put it upon the horns of the altar round about. [19] And he shall sprinkle of the _____upon it with

his finger seven times, and cleanse it, and _____ it from the _____ of the children of Israel.

[20] And when he hath made an end of _____ the holy place, and the tabernacle of the congregation, and the altar, he shall bring the _____ goat: [21] And Aaron shall lay _____ his _____ upon the _____ of the _____ goat, and _____ over him _____ the _____ of the children of Israel, and _____ their _____ in _____ their _____, putting them upon the _____ of the _____, and shall send him away by the _____ of a _____ man into the _____: [22] And the goat shall _____ upon him all their _____ unto a _____ not inhabited: and he shall let go the goat in the wilderness. [23] And Aaron shall come into the tabernacle of the congregation, and shall put off the linen garments, which he put on when he went into the holy place, and shall leave them there: [24] And he shall wash his flesh with water in the holy place, and put on his garments, and come forth, and offer his burnt offering, and the burnt offering of the people, and make an atonement for himself, and for the people. [25] And the fat of the sin offering shall he burn upon the altar. [26] And he that let go the goat for the scapegoat shall wash his clothes, and bathe his flesh in water, and afterward come into the camp. [27] And the bullock for the sin offering, and the goat for the sin offering, whose blood was brought in to make atonement in the holy place, shall one carry forth without the camp; and they shall burn in the fire their skins, and their flesh, and their dung. [28] And he that burneth them shall wash his clothes, and bathe his flesh in water, and afterward he shall come into the camp.

[29] And this shall be a _____ for ever unto you: that in the _____ month, on the _____ day of the month, ye shall _____ your souls, and do no _____ at all, whether it be one of your own country, or a stranger that sojourneth among you: [30] For on that day shall the priest make an atonement for you, to cleanse you, that ye may be clean from all your sins before the Lord. [31] _____ shall be a _____ of rest unto you, and ye shall afflict your souls, by a statute for ever. [32] And the priest, whom he shall _____, and whom he shall _____ to minister in the priest's office in his father's stead, shall make the atonement, and shall put on the linen clothes, even the holy garments: [33] And he shall make an atonement for the holy _____, and he shall make an atonement for the _____ of the congregation, and for the _____, and he shall make an atonement for the _____, and for all the _____ of the congregation. [34] And this shall be an everlasting statute unto you, to make an atonement for the children of Israel for all their sins _____ a _____. And he did as the Lord commanded Moses.

[17:1] And the Lord spake unto Moses, saying, [2] Speak unto Aaron, and unto his sons, and unto all the children of Israel, and say unto them; This is the thing which the Lord hath commanded, saying, [3] What man soever there be of the house of Israel, that killeth an ox, or lamb, or goat, in the camp, or that killeth it out of the camp, [4] And bringeth it not unto the door of the tabernacle of the congregation, to offer an offering unto the Lord before the tabernacle of the Lord; blood shall be imputed unto that man; he hath shed blood; and that man shall be cut off from among his people: [5] To the end that the children of Israel may bring their sacrifices, which they offer in the open field, even that they may bring them unto the Lord, unto the door of the tabernacle of the congregation, unto the priest, and offer them for _____ offerings unto the Lord. [6] And the priest shall sprinkle the blood upon the altar of the Lord at the door of the tabernacle of the congregation, and burn the fat for a sweet savour unto the Lord. [7] And they shall no more offer their sacrifices unto _____, after whom they have gone a whoring. This shall be a statute for ever unto them throughout their generations.

[8] And thou shalt say unto them, Whatsoever man there be of the house of Israel, or of the strangers which sojourn among you, that offereth a burnt offering of sacrifice, [9] And bringeth it not unto the door of the tabernacle of the congregation, to offer it unto the _____; even that man shall be cut off from among his people.

[10] And whatsoever man there be of the house of Israel, or of the strangers that sojourn among you, that _____ any manner of _____; I will even set my face against that soul that eateth blood, and will cut him off from among his people. [11] For the _____ of the _____ is in the _____: and I have given it to you upon the altar to make an atonement for your souls: for it is the _____ that maketh an _____ for the _____. [12] Therefore I said unto the children of Israel, No soul of you shall eat blood, neither shall any stranger that sojourneth among you eat blood. [13] And whatsoever man there be of the children of Israel, or of the strangers that sojourn among you, which _____ and _____ any _____ or _____ that may be _____; he shall even pour _____ the _____ thereof, and _____ it with _____. [14] For it is the _____ of all _____; the _____ of it is for the _____ thereof: therefore I said unto the children of Israel, Ye shall eat the blood of no manner of flesh: for the life of all flesh is the blood thereof: whosoever eateth it shall be cut off. [15] And every soul that eateth that which died of itself, or that which was torn with beasts, whether it be one of your own country, or a stranger, he shall both wash his clothes, and bathe himself in water, and be unclean until the even: then shall he be clean. [16] But if he wash them not, nor bathe his flesh; then he shall bear his iniquity.

[18:1] And the Lord spake unto Moses, saying, [2] Speak unto the children of Israel, and say unto them, I am the _____ your _____. [3] After the _____ of the land of _____, wherein ye dwelt, shall ye _____ do: and after the doings of the land of _____, whither I bring you, shall ye _____ do: neither shall ye _____ in their _____. [4] Ye shall do _____ judgments, and keep _____ ordinances, to _____ therein: I am the _____ your _____. [5] Ye shall therefore keep my _____, and my _____: which if a man _____, he shall _____ in them: I am the _____.

[6] None of you shall approach to any that is near of kin to him, to uncover their _____: I am the Lord. [7] The nakedness of thy _____, or the nakedness of thy _____, shalt thou not _____: she is thy _____; thou shalt _____ uncover her nakedness. [8] The nakedness of thy father's _____ shalt thou _____ uncover: it is thy _____ nakedness. [9] The nakedness of thy _____, the daughter of thy father, or daughter of thy mother, whether she be born at home, or born abroad, even their nakedness thou shalt not uncover. [10] The nakedness of thy son's _____, or of thy daughter's _____, even their nakedness thou shalt _____ uncover: for theirs is thine own nakedness. [11] The nakedness of thy father's wife's _____, begotten of thy father, she is thy _____, thou shalt

LEVITICUS

_____ uncover her _____. [12] Thou shalt not uncover the nakedness of thy father's _____: she is thy father's near kinswoman. [13] Thou shalt not uncover the nakedness of thy mother's _____: for she is thy mother's near kinswoman. [14] Thou shalt not uncover the nakedness of thy father's _____, thou shalt not approach to his _____: she is thine _____. [15] Thou shalt not uncover the nakedness of thy _____ in _____: she is thy son's _____; thou shalt not uncover her _____. [16] Thou shalt not uncover the nakedness of thy brother's _____: it is thy brother's nakedness. [17] Thou shalt not uncover the nakedness of a _____ and her _____, neither shalt thou take her son's daughter, or her daughter's daughter, to uncover her _____; for they are her near kinswomen: it is _____. [18] Neither shalt thou take a _____ to her _____, to _____ her, to uncover her nakedness, beside the other in her _____ time. [19] Also thou shalt not approach unto a woman to uncover her nakedness, as long as she is put apart for her uncleanness. [20] Moreover thou shalt not lie _____ with thy neighbour's _____, to _____ thyself with her. [21] And thou shalt not let any of thy _____ pass through the _____ to _____, neither shalt thou _____ the _____ of thy _____: I am the _____. [22] Thou shalt not _____ with _____, as with _____: it is _____. [23] Neither shalt thou _____ with any _____ to defile thyself therewith: neither shall any woman stand before a beast to lie down thereto: it is _____. [24] Defile not ye yourselves in _____ of these things: for in all these the nations are defiled which I cast out before you: [25] And the land is defiled: therefore I do visit the iniquity thereof upon it, and the land itself _____ out her _____. [26] Ye shall therefore _____ my statutes and my judgments, and shall _____ commit any of these _____; neither any of your own nation, nor any stranger that sojourneth among you: [27] (For all these abominations have the men of the land done, which were before you, and the land is _____;) [28] That the land spue not you out also, when ye defile it, as it spued out the nations that were before you. [29] For whosoever shall commit any of these abominations, even the souls that commit them shall be cut off from among their people. [30] Therefore shall ye _____ mine _____, that ye commit not any one of these abominable customs, which were committed before you, and that ye defile not yourselves therein: I am the Lord your God.

[19:1] And the Lord spake unto Moses, saying, [2] Speak unto all the congregation of the children of Israel, and say unto them, Ye shall be _____: for I the Lord your God am _____.

[3] Ye shall _____ every man his _____, and his _____, and keep my _____: I am the Lord your _____.

[4] Turn ye _____ unto _____, nor make to yourselves _____ gods: I am the Lord your God.

[5] And if ye offer a sacrifice of peace offerings unto the Lord, ye shall offer it at your own _____. [6] It shall be eaten the _____ day ye offer it, and on the morrow: and if ought remain until the third day, it shall be burnt in the fire. [7] And if it be eaten at all on the third day, it is abominable; it shall not be accepted. [8] Therefore every one that eateth it shall bear his iniquity, because he hath _____ the _____ thing of the Lord: and that soul shall be cut off from among his people.

[9] And when ye _____ the _____ of your land, thou shalt not _____reap the _____ of thy field, neither shalt thou gather the _____ of thy harvest. [10] And thou shalt not glean thy vineyard, neither shalt thou gather _____grape of thy vineyard; thou shalt _____them for the _____and _____: I am the Lord your God.

[11] Ye shall not _____, neither _____falsely, neither _____one to another.

[12] And ye shall not swear by my name _____, neither shalt thou profane the name of thy God: I am the Lord.

[13] Thou shalt not _____thy neighbour, neither _____him: the wages of him that is _____shall not _____with thee all _____until the _____.

[14] Thou shalt not _____the _____, nor put a stumblingblock before the _____, but shalt _____thy God: I am the Lord.

[15] Ye shall do no _____in judgment: thou shalt not _____the person of the _____, nor honour the person of the mighty: but in _____shalt thou _____thy neighbour.

[16] Thou shalt not go up and down as a _____among thy people: neither shalt thou stand against the blood of thy neighbour: I am the Lord.

[17] Thou shalt not _____thy brother in thine _____: thou shalt in any wise rebuke thy neighbour, and not suffer sin upon him.

[18] Thou shalt not _____, nor bear any _____against the children of thy people, but thou shalt _____thy _____as thyself: I am the Lord.

[19] Ye shall keep my statutes. Thou shalt not let thy _____gender with a diverse _____: thou shalt not _____thy field with _____seed: neither shall a garment mingled of linen and woollen come upon thee.

[20] And whosoever lieth _____with a woman, that is a _____, betrothed to an husband, and not at all redeemed, nor freedom given her; she shall be _____; they shall not be put to death, because she was not free. [21] And he shall bring his trespass offering unto the Lord, unto the door of the tabernacle of the congregation, even a ram for a trespass offering. [22] And the priest shall make an _____for him with the ram of the trespass offering before the Lord for his sin which he hath done: and the _____which he hath done shall be _____him.

[23] And when ye shall come into the land, and shall have _____all manner of _____for _____, then ye shall count the fruit thereof as uncircumcised: three years shall it be as uncircumcised unto you: it shall not be eaten of. [24] But in the fourth year all the fruit thereof shall be holy to praise the Lord withal. [25] And in the _____year shall ye eat of the fruit thereof, that it may yield unto you the increase thereof: I am the Lord your God.

[26] Ye shall not eat any thing with the _____: neither shall ye use _____, nor observe _____. [27] Ye shall not _____the _____of your _____, neither shalt thou mar the _____of thy _____. [28] Ye shall not make any _____in your _____for the dead, nor _____any _____upon you: I am the _____.

[29] Do not _____thy _____, to cause her to be a _____; lest the land fall to whoredom, and the land become full of _____.

LEVITICUS

[30] Ye shall keep my _____, and reverence my _____: I am the Lord.

[31] Regard _____ them that have familiar _____, neither seek after _____, to be defiled by them: I am the Lord your God.

[32] Thou shalt _____ up before the _____ head, and _____ the _____ of the _____ man, and fear thy God: I am the Lord.

[33] And if a stranger sojourn with thee in your land, ye shall not _____ him. [34] But the stranger that dwelleth with you shall be unto you as one born among you, and thou shalt love him as thyself; for ye were strangers in the land of Egypt: I am the Lord your God.

[35] Ye shall do no unrighteousness in judgment, in meteyard, in _____, or in _____. [36] Just _____, just _____, a just ephah, and a just hin, shall ye have: I am the Lord your God, which brought you out of the land of Egypt. [37] Therefore shall ye observe all my statutes, and all my judgments, and do them: I am the Lord.

[20:1] And the Lord spake unto Moses, saying, [2] Again, thou shalt say to the children of Israel, Whosoever he be of the children of Israel, or of the strangers that sojourn in Israel, that giveth any of his seed unto Molech; he shall surely be put to _____: the people of the land shall stone him with stones. [3] And I will set my face against that man, and will cut him off from among his people; because he hath given of his seed unto Molech, to defile my sanctuary, and to profane my holy name. [4] And if the people of the land do any ways hide their eyes from the man, when he giveth of his seed unto Molech, and kill him not: [5] Then I will set my face against that man, and against his family, and will cut him off, and all that go a whoring after him, to commit whoredom with Molech, from among their people.

[6] And the soul that turneth after such as have familiar _____, and after _____, to go a whoring after them, I will even set my face against that soul, and will cut him off from among his people.

[7] _____ yourselves therefore, and be ye _____: for I am the Lord your God. [8] And ye shall keep my statutes, and do them: I am the Lord which sanctify you.

[9] For every one that _____ his _____ or his _____ shall be surely put to _____: he hath cursed his father or his mother; his blood shall be upon him.

[10] And the man that committeth _____ with another man's _____, even he that committeth adultery with his neighbour's wife, the _____ and the _____ shall surely be put to _____. [11] And the man that _____ with his father's _____ hath uncovered his father's nakedness: both of them shall surely be put to _____; their blood shall be upon them. [12] And if a man lie with his _____ in _____, both of them shall surely be put to _____: they have wrought _____; their blood shall be upon them. [13] If a man also lie with _____, as he lieth with a _____, both of them have _____ an _____: they shall surely be put to _____; their blood shall be upon them. [14] And if a man take a _____ and her _____, it is _____: they shall be _____ with _____, both he and they; that there be no wickedness among you. [15] And if a _____ lie with a _____, he shall surely be put to _____: and ye shall slay the beast. [16] And if a woman approach unto any beast, and lie down thereto, thou shalt _____ the woman, and

the _____: they shall surely be put to death; their blood shall be upon them. [17] And if a man shall take his _____, his father's _____, or his mother's _____, and see her _____, and she see his _____; it is a _____thing; and they shall be cut off in the sight of their people: he hath uncovered his sister's nakedness; he shall bear his iniquity. [18] And if a man shall lie with a woman having her sickness, and shall uncover her nakedness; he hath discovered her fountain, and she hath uncovered the fountain of her blood: and both of them shall be cut off from among their people. [19] And thou shalt not uncover the nakedness of thy mother's sister, nor of thy father's sister: for he uncovereth his near kin: they shall bear their iniquity. [20] And if a man shall lie with his uncle's wife, he hath uncovered his uncle's nakedness: they shall bear their sin; they shall die _____. [21] And if a man shall take his brother's wife, it is an unclean thing: he hath uncovered his brother's nakedness; they shall be _____.

[22] Ye shall therefore keep all my statutes, and all my judgments, and do them: that the land, whither I bring you to dwell therein, spue you not out. [23] And ye shall not walk in the manners of the nation, which I cast out before you: for they _____all these _____, and therefore I _____them. [24] But I have said unto you, Ye shall inherit their land, and I will give it unto you to possess it, a land that floweth with _____ and _____: I am the Lord your God, which have separated you from other people. [25] Ye shall therefore put difference between _____beasts and _____, and between unclean fowls and clean: and ye shall not make your souls abominable by beast, or by fowl, or by any manner of living thing that creepeth on the ground, which I have separated from you as unclean. [26] And ye shall be holy unto me: for I the Lord am holy, and have severed you from other people, that ye should be mine.

[27] A man also or woman that hath a familiar _____, or that is a _____, shall surely be put to _____: they shall _____them with _____: their blood shall be upon them.

[21:1] And the Lord said unto Moses, Speak unto the priests the sons of Aaron, and say unto them, There shall none be defiled for the dead among his people: [2] But for his kin, that is near unto him, that is, for his mother, and for his father, and for his son, and for his daughter, and for his brother, [3] And for his sister a _____, that is nigh unto him, which hath had no husband; for her may he be defiled. [4] But he shall not defile himself, being a chief man among his people, to profane himself. [5] They shall not make _____upon their head, neither shall they _____off the _____of their _____, nor make any _____in their _____. [6] They shall be holy unto their God, and not _____the _____of their God: for the offerings of the Lord made by _____, and the _____of their God, they do offer: therefore they shall be _____. [7] They shall not take a _____that is a _____, or profane; neither shall they take a woman put away from her husband: for he is holy unto his God. [8] Thou shalt sanctify him therefore; for he offereth the bread of thy God: he shall be holy unto thee: for I the Lord, which sanctify you, am holy.

[9] And the _____of any priest, if she profane herself by playing the _____, she _____her _____: she shall be burnt with _____. [10] And he that is the high priest among his brethren, upon whose head the anointing _____was poured, and that is consecrated to put on the garments, shall not uncover his head, nor rend his clothes; [11] Neither shall he go in to any dead body, nor

LEVITICUS

defile himself for his father, or for his mother; [12] Neither shall he go out of the sanctuary, nor profane the sanctuary of his God; for the crown of the anointing oil of his God is upon him: I am the Lord. [13] And he shall take a _____ in her _____. [14] A _____, or a _____ woman, or _____, or an _____, these shall he _____ take: but he shall take a _____ of his _____ people to _____. [15] Neither shall he profane his seed among his people: for I the Lord do sanctify him.

   [16] And the Lord spake unto Moses, saying, [17] Speak unto Aaron, saying, Whosoever he be of thy seed in their generations that hath any _____, let him not approach to offer the bread of his God. [18] For whatsoever man he be that hath a blemish, he shall not approach: a _____ man, or a _____, or he that hath a flat _____, or any thing _____, [19] Or a man that is _____, or _____, [20] Or _____, or a _____, or that hath a _____ in his _____, or be _____, or _____, or hath his stones _____; [21] No man that hath a blemish of the seed of Aaron the priest shall come nigh to offer the offerings of the Lord made by fire: he hath a blemish; he shall not come nigh to offer the bread of his God. [22] He shall eat the bread of his God, both of the most holy, and of the holy. [23] Only he shall not go in unto the _____, nor come nigh unto the _____, because he hath a _____; that he profane not my sanctuaries: for I the Lord do _____ them. [24] And Moses told it unto Aaron, and to his sons, and unto all the children of Israel.

   [22:1] And the Lord spake unto Moses, saying, [2] Speak unto Aaron and to his sons, that they _____ themselves from the holy things of the children of Israel, and that they profane not my holy name in those things which they hallow unto me: I am the Lord. [3] Say unto them, Whosoever he be of all your seed among your generations, that goeth unto the holy things, which the children of Israel hallow unto the Lord, having his uncleanness upon him, that soul shall be cut off from my presence: I am the Lord. [4] What man soever of the seed of Aaron is a _____, or hath a running _____; he shall not eat of the holy things, until he be clean. And whoso toucheth any thing that is unclean by the dead, or a man whose seed goeth from him; [5] Or whosoever toucheth any creeping thing, whereby he may be made unclean, or a man of whom he may take uncleanness, whatsoever uncleanness he hath; [6] The soul which hath touched any such shall be unclean until even, and shall not eat of the holy things, unless he wash his flesh with water. [7] And when the _____ is down, he shall be clean, and shall afterward eat of the holy things; because it is his _____. [8] That which dieth of itself, or is torn with beasts, he shall not eat to defile himself therewith: I am the Lord. [9] They shall therefore keep mine ordinance, lest they bear sin for it, and die therefore, if they profane it: I the Lord do sanctify them. [10] There shall no stranger eat of the holy thing: a sojourner of the priest, or an hired servant, shall not eat of the holy thing. [11] But if the priest _____ any soul with his _____, he shall eat of it, and he that is _____ in his house: they shall eat of his _____. [12] If the priest's _____ also be married unto a _____, she may _____ eat of an offering of the holy things. [13] But if the priest's _____ be a _____, or _____, and have no _____, and is returned unto her father's _____, as in her _____, she shall eat of her father's _____: but there shall no stranger eat thereof.

28

LEVITICUS

[14] And if a man eat of the holy thing _____, then he shall put the _____ part thereof unto it, and shall give it unto the priest with the holy thing. [15] And they shall not profane the holy things of the children of Israel, which they offer unto the Lord; [16] Or suffer them to bear the iniquity of trespass, when they eat their holy things: for I the Lord do sanctify them.

[17] And the Lord spake unto Moses, saying, [18] Speak unto Aaron, and to his sons, and unto all the children of Israel, and say unto them, Whatsoever he be of the house of Israel, or of the strangers in Israel, that will offer his oblation for all his vows, and for all his freewill offerings, which they will offer unto the Lord for a burnt offering; [19] Ye shall offer at your own will a male without blemish, of the _____, of the sheep, or of the goats. [20] But whatsoever hath a blemish, that shall ye not offer: for it shall not be acceptable for you. [21] And whosoever offereth a sacrifice of peace offerings unto the Lord to accomplish his vow, or a freewill offering in beeves or _____, it shall be _____ to be _____; there shall be _____ blemish therein. [22] _____, or _____, or _____, or having a _____, or _____, or _____, ye shall not offer these unto the Lord, nor make an offering by fire of them upon the altar unto the Lord. [23] Either a bullock or a lamb that hath any thing _____ or _____ in his parts, that mayest thou offer for a _____ offering; but for a _____ it shall not be _____. [24] Ye shall not offer unto the Lord that which is bruised, or crushed, or broken, or cut; neither shall ye make any offering thereof in your land. [25] Neither from a stranger's hand shall ye offer the bread of your God of any of these; because their corruption is in them, and blemishes be in them: they shall not be accepted for you.

[26] And the Lord spake unto Moses, saying, [27] When a bullock, or a sheep, or a goat, is brought forth, then it shall be seven days under the dam; and from the eighth day and thenceforth it shall be accepted for an offering made by fire unto the Lord. [28] And whether it be cow or ewe, ye shall not kill it and her young both in one day. [29] And when ye will offer a sacrifice of thanksgiving unto the Lord, offer it at your own will. [30] On the same day it shall be eaten up; ye shall leave none of it until the morrow: I am the Lord. [31] Therefore shall ye _____ my _____, and _____ them: I am the Lord. [32] Neither shall ye profane my holy name; but I will be hallowed among the children of Israel: I am the Lord which hallow you, [33] That brought you out of the land of Egypt, to be your God: I am the Lord.

[23:1] And the Lord spake unto Moses, saying, [2] Speak unto the children of Israel, and say unto them, Concerning the _____ of the Lord, which ye shall proclaim to be holy convocations, even these are _____ feasts. [3] _____ days shall work be done: but the seventh day is the _____ of rest, an holy _____; ye shall do no work therein: it is the sabbath of the Lord in all your dwellings.

[4] These are the feasts of the Lord, even holy convocations, which ye shall proclaim in their seasons. [5] In the _____ day of the _____ month at even is the Lord's _____. [6] And on the _____ day of the _____ month is the feast of _____ bread unto the Lord: seven days ye must eat unleavened bread. [7] In the first day ye shall have an holy convocation: ye shall do no servile work therein. [8] But ye shall offer an offering made by fire unto the Lord seven days: in the seventh day is an holy convocation: ye shall do no servile work therein.

[9] And the Lord spake unto Moses, saying, [10] Speak unto the children of Israel, and say unto them, When ye be come into the land which I give unto you, and shall reap the harvest thereof, then ye shall bring a sheaf of the _____ of your harvest unto the priest: [11] And he shall wave the sheaf before the Lord, to be accepted for you: on the morrow after the sabbath the priest shall wave it. [12] And ye shall offer that day when ye wave the sheaf an he lamb without blemish of the first year for a burnt offering unto the Lord. [13] And the meat offering thereof shall be two tenth deals of fine flour mingled with oil, an offering made by fire unto the Lord for a sweet savour: and the drink offering thereof shall be of wine, the fourth part of an hin. [14] And ye shall eat neither bread, nor parched corn, nor green ears, until the selfsame day that ye have brought an offering unto your God: it shall be a statute for ever throughout your generations in all your dwellings.

[15] And ye shall count unto you from the morrow after the sabbath, from the day that ye brought the sheaf of the wave offering; seven sabbaths shall be complete: [16] Even unto the _____ after the seventh sabbath shall ye number _____ days; and ye shall offer a new meat offering unto the Lord. [17] Ye shall bring out of your habitations two wave loaves of two tenth deals: they shall be of fine flour; they shall be baken _____ leaven; they are the _____ unto the Lord. [18] And ye shall offer with the _____ seven lambs without blemish of the first year, and one young bullock, and two rams: they shall be for a burnt offering unto the Lord, with their meat offering, and their drink offerings, even an offering made by fire, of sweet savour unto the Lord. [19] Then ye shall sacrifice one kid of the goats for a sin offering, and two lambs of the first year for a sacrifice of peace offerings. [20] And the priest shall wave them with the bread of the first fruits for a wave offering before the Lord, with the two lambs: they shall be holy to the Lord for the priest. [21] And ye shall proclaim on the selfsame day, that it may be an holy _____ unto you: ye shall do no servile work therein: it shall be a statute for ever in all your dwellings throughout your generations.

[22] And when ye _____ the harvest of your land, thou shalt not make clean riddance of the _____ of thy field when thou reapest, neither shalt thou gather any _____ of thy harvest: thou shalt leave them unto the _____, and to the _____: I am the Lord your God.

[23] And the Lord spake unto Moses, saying, [24] Speak unto the children of Israel, saying, In the _____ month, in the _____ day of the month, shall ye have a _____, a memorial of blowing of _____, an holy convocation. [25] Ye shall do no servile work therein: but ye shall offer an offering made by fire unto the Lord.

[26] And the Lord spake unto Moses, saying, [27] Also on the tenth day of this seventh month there shall be a day of atonement: it shall be an holy convocation unto you; and ye shall afflict your souls, and offer an offering made by fire unto the Lord. [28] And ye shall do no work in that same day: for it is a day of atonement, to make an atonement for you before the Lord your God. [29] For whatsoever soul it be that shall not be afflicted in that same day, he shall be cut off from among his people. [30] And whatsoever soul it be that doeth any work in that same day, the same soul will I destroy from among his people. [31] Ye shall do no manner of work: it shall be a statute for ever throughout your generations in all your dwellings. [32] It shall be unto you a sabbath of rest, and ye shall afflict your souls: in the ninth day of the month at even, from even unto even, shall ye celebrate your sabbath.

LEVITICUS

[33] And the Lord spake unto Moses, saying, [34] Speak unto the children of Israel, saying, The fifteenth day of this seventh month shall be the feast of tabernacles for seven days unto the Lord. [35] On the first day shall be an holy convocation: ye shall do no servile work therein. [36] Seven days ye shall offer an offering made by fire unto the Lord: on the _____ day shall be an holy convocation unto you; and ye shall offer an offering made by fire unto the Lord: it is a _____ assembly; and ye shall do no servile work therein. [37] These are the _____ of the Lord, which ye shall proclaim to be holy convocations, to offer an offering made by fire unto the Lord, a burnt offering, and a meat offering, a sacrifice, and drink offerings, every thing upon his day: [38] Beside the sabbaths of the Lord, and beside your gifts, and beside all your vows, and beside all your freewill offerings, which ye give unto the Lord. [39] Also in the _____ day of the seventh month, when ye have gathered in the fruit of the land, ye shall keep a feast unto the Lord seven days: on the _____ day shall be a _____, and on the _____ day shall be a _____. [40] And ye shall take you on the first day the boughs of goodly trees, branches of palm trees, and the boughs of thick trees, and willows of the brook; and ye shall rejoice before the Lord your God seven days. [41] And ye shall keep it a feast unto the Lord seven days in the year. It shall be a statute for ever in your generations: ye shall celebrate it in the seventh month. [42] Ye shall _____ in _____ seven days; all that are Israelites born shall dwell in booths: [43] That your generations may know that I made the children of Israel to dwell in booths, when I brought them out of the land of Egypt: I am the Lord your God. [44] And Moses declared unto the children of Israel the feasts of the Lord.

[24:1] And the Lord spake unto Moses, saying, [2] Command the children of Israel, that they bring unto thee pure _____ olive beaten for the light, to cause the lamps to burn continually. [3] Without the vail of the testimony, in the tabernacle of the congregation, shall Aaron order it from the evening unto the morning before the Lord continually: it shall be a statute for ever in your generations. [4] He shall order the lamps upon the pure candlestick before the Lord continually.

[5] And thou shalt take fine flour, and bake twelve cakes thereof: two tenth deals shall be in one cake. [6] And thou shalt set them in two rows, six on a row, upon the pure table before the Lord. [7] And thou shalt put pure frankincense upon each row, that it may be on the bread for a memorial, even an offering made by fire unto the Lord. [8] Every sabbath he shall set it in _____ before the Lord continually, being taken from the children of Israel by an everlasting covenant. [9] And it shall be Aaron's and his sons'; and they shall eat it in the holy place: for it is most holy unto him of the offerings of the Lord made by fire by a perpetual statute.

[10] And the _____ of an _____ woman, whose _____ was an _____, went out among the children of Israel: and this son of the Israelitish woman and a _____ of Israel _____ together in the _____; [11] And the Israelitish woman's son _____ the name of the _____, and _____. And they brought him unto Moses: (and his mother's name was Shelomith, the daughter of Dibri, of the tribe of Dan:) [12] And they put him in ward, that the _____ of the Lord might be shewed them. [13] And the Lord spake unto Moses, saying, [14] Bring forth him that hath cursed without the camp; and let all that heard him lay their hands upon his head, and let all the congregation _____ him. [15] And thou shalt speak unto the children of Israel, saying, Whosoever _____ his God

shall _____ his sin. [16] And he that blasphemeth the name of the Lord, he shall surely be put to _____, and all the congregation shall certainly stone him: as well the _____, as he that is born in the land, when he _____ the name of the _____, shall be put to _____.

[17] And he that _____ any man shall surely be put to death. [18] And he that killeth a _____ shall make it _____; beast for beast. [19] And if a man cause a blemish in his _____; as he hath done, so shall it be done to him; [20] _____ for _____, _____ for _____, _____ for _____: as he hath caused a blemish in a man, so shall it be done to him again. [21] And he that killeth a beast, he shall _____ it: and he that killeth a man, he shall be put to _____. [22] Ye shall have one manner of law, as well for the stranger, as for one of your own country: for I am the Lord your God.

[23] And Moses spake to the children of Israel, that they should bring forth him that had cursed out of the camp, and stone him with stones. And the children of Israel _____ as the Lord commanded Moses.

[25:1] And the Lord spake unto Moses in mount Sinai, saying, [2] Speak unto the children of Israel, and say unto them, When ye come into the land which I give you, then shall the land keep a _____ unto the Lord. [3] Six years thou shalt sow thy field, and six years thou shalt prune thy vineyard, and gather in the fruit thereof; [4] But in the _____ year shall be a _____ of rest unto the land, a sabbath for the Lord: thou shalt neither sow thy field, nor prune thy vineyard. [5] That which _____ of its own accord of thy harvest thou shalt _____ reap, neither gather the grapes of thy vine undressed: for it is a year of rest unto the land. [6] And the sabbath of the land shall be meat for you; for thee, and for thy servant, and for thy maid, and for thy hired servant, and for thy stranger that sojourneth with thee, [7] And for thy cattle, and for the beast that are in thy land, shall all the increase thereof be meat.

[8] And thou shalt number _____ sabbaths of years unto thee, _____ times _____ years; and the space of the seven sabbaths of years shall be unto thee forty and nine years. [9] Then shalt thou cause the trumpet of the _____ to sound on the tenth day of the seventh month, in the _____ of _____ shall ye make the trumpet sound throughout all your land. [10] And ye shall _____ the _____ year, and proclaim _____ throughout all the _____ unto all the inhabitants thereof: it shall be a _____ unto you; and ye shall return every man unto his _____, and ye shall return every man unto his _____. [11] A _____ shall that _____ year be unto you: ye shall not sow, neither reap that which groweth of itself in it, nor gather the grapes in it of thy vine undressed. [12] For it is the _____; it shall be holy unto you: ye shall eat the increase thereof out of the field. [13] In the _____ of this _____ ye shall return every man unto his possession. [14] And if thou sell ought unto thy neighbour, or buyest ought of thy neighbour's hand, ye shall not oppress one another: [15] According to the number of years after the _____ thou shalt buy of thy neighbour, and according unto the number of years of the fruits he shall sell unto thee: [16] According to the _____ of years thou shalt _____ the _____ thereof, and according to the _____ of years thou shalt _____ the _____ of it: for according to the number of the years of the fruits doth he _____ unto thee. [17] Ye shall not

therefore _____ one another; but thou shalt _____ thy _____ : for I am the Lord your God.

[18] Wherefore ye shall do my _____ , and keep my _____ , and do them; and ye shall dwell in the land in _____ . [19] And the land shall _____ her _____ , and ye shall eat your _____ , and dwell therein in _____ . [20] And if ye shall say, What shall we eat the seventh year? behold, we shall not sow, nor gather in our increase: [21] Then I will _____ my _____ upon you in the sixth year, and it shall bring forth fruit for three years. [22] And ye shall sow the eighth year, and eat yet of old fruit until the ninth year; until her fruits come in ye shall eat of the old store.

[23] The land shall not be _____ for ever: for the land is _____ ; for ye are strangers and sojourners with me. [24] And in all the land of your possession ye shall grant a redemption for the land.

[25] If thy brother be waxen poor, and hath sold away some of his possession, and if any of his kin come to redeem it, then shall he redeem that which his brother sold. [26] And if the man have none to redeem it, and himself be able to redeem it; [27] Then let him count the years of the sale thereof, and restore the overplus unto the man to whom he sold it; that he may return unto his possession. [28] But if he be not able to restore it to him, then that which is sold shall remain in the hand of him that hath bought it until the year of jubile: and in the jubile it shall go out, and he shall return unto his possession. [29] And if a man sell a dwelling house in a walled city, then he may redeem it within a whole year after it is sold; within a full year may he redeem it. [30] And if it be not redeemed within the space of a full year, then the house that is in the walled city shall be established for ever to him that bought it throughout his generations: it shall not go out in the jubile. [31] But the houses of the villages which have no wall round about them shall be counted as the fields of the country: they may be redeemed, and they shall go out in the jubile. [32] Notwithstanding the cities of the _____ , and the houses of the cities of their possession, may the Levites _____ at _____ time. [33] And if a man purchase of the Levites, then the house that was sold, and the city of his possession, shall go out in the year of jubile: for the houses of the cities of the Levites are their possession among the children of Israel. [34] But the field of the suburbs of their cities may not be sold; for it is their perpetual possession.

[35] And if thy brother be waxen poor, and fallen in decay with thee; then thou shalt relieve him: yea, though he be a stranger, or a sojourner; that he may live with thee. [36] Take thou no _____ of him, or _____ : but fear thy God; that thy brother may live with thee. [37] Thou shalt not give him thy money upon usury, nor lend him thy victuals for increase. [38] I am the Lord your God, which brought you forth out of the land of Egypt, to give you the land of Canaan, and to be your God.

[39] And if thy brother that dwelleth by thee be waxen poor, and be sold unto thee; thou shalt not compel him to serve as a bondservant: [40] But as an hired servant, and as a sojourner, he shall be with thee, and shall serve thee unto the year of jubile: [41] And then shall he depart from thee, both he and his children with him, and shall return unto his own family, and unto the possession of his fathers shall he return. [42] For they are my servants, which I brought forth out of the land of Egypt: they shall not be sold as bondmen. [43] Thou shalt not rule over him with _____ ; but shalt fear thy God. [44] Both thy bondmen, and thy bondmaids, which thou shalt have, shall be of the

heathen that are round about you; of them shall ye buy bondmen and bondmaids. [45] Moreover of the children of the strangers that do sojourn among you, of them shall ye buy, and of their families that are with you, which they begat in your land: and they shall be your possession. [46] And ye shall take them as an inheritance for your children after you, to inherit them for a possession; they shall be your bondmen for ever: but over your brethren the children of Israel, ye shall not rule one over another with rigour.

[47] And if a sojourner or stranger wax rich by thee, and thy brother that dwelleth by him wax poor, and sell himself unto the stranger or sojourner by thee, or to the stock of the stranger's family: [48] After that he is sold he may be redeemed again; one of his brethren may redeem him: [49] Either his uncle, or his uncle's son, may redeem him, or any that is nigh of kin unto him of his family may redeem him; or if he be able, he may redeem himself. [50] And he shall reckon with him that bought him from the year that he was sold to him unto the year of jubile: and the price of his sale shall be according unto the number of years, according to the time of an hired servant shall it be with him. [51] If there be yet many years behind, according unto them he shall give again the price of his redemption out of the money that he was bought for. [52] And if there remain but few years unto the year of jubile, then he shall count with him, and according unto his years shall he give him again the price of his redemption. [53] And as a yearly hired servant shall he be with him: and the other shall not rule with rigour over him in thy sight. [54] And if he be not redeemed in these years, then he shall go out in the year of jubile, both he, and his children with him. [55] For unto me the children of Israel are _____; they are _____ servants whom I brought forth out of the land of Egypt: I am the Lord your God.

[26:1] Ye shall make you no _____ nor graven _____, neither rear you up a standing _____, neither shall ye set up any image of _____ in your land, _____ bow _____ unto it: for I am the Lord your God.

[2] Ye shall _____ my sabbaths, and _____ my _____: I am the Lord.

[3] If ye _____ in my _____, and _____ my _____, and _____ them; [4] Then I will _____ you _____ in due season, and the land shall yield her _____, and the trees of the field shall yield their _____. [5] And your threshing shall reach unto the vintage, and the vintage shall reach unto the sowing time: and ye shall eat your bread to the _____, and dwell in your land _____. [6] And I will give _____ in the land, and ye shall lie down, and none shall make you _____: and I will rid evil beasts out of the land, neither shall the _____ go through your land. [7] And ye shall chase your _____, and they shall fall before you by the sword. [8] And _____ of you shall chase an _____, and an hundred of you shall put _____ thousand to flight: and your enemies shall fall before you by the sword. [9] For I will have _____ unto you, and make you fruitful, and multiply you, and establish my covenant with you. [10] And ye shall eat old store, and bring forth the old because of the new. [11] And I will set my _____ among you: and my _____ shall not abhor you. [12] And I will _____ among you, and will be your God, and ye shall be my people. [13] I am the Lord your God, which brought you forth out of the land of Egypt, that ye should not be their bondmen; and I have _____ the bands of your _____, and made you go _____.

LEVITICUS

[14] But if ye will _____ hearken unto me, and will _____ do all these _____ ; [15] And if ye shall _____ my statutes, or if your soul _____ my _____ , so that ye will _____ do all my commandments, but that ye _____ my covenant: [16] I also _____ do this unto you; I will even _____ over you _____ , consumption, and the burning ague, that shall consume the eyes, and cause _____ of heart: and ye shall sow your seed in vain, for your enemies shall eat it. [17] And I will set my face against you, and ye shall be slain before your enemies: they that hate you shall reign over you; and ye shall flee when none pursueth you. [18] And if ye will not yet for all this hearken unto me, then I will _____ you seven times more for your sins. [19] And I will break the _____ of your power; and I will make your _____ as _____ , and your _____ as _____ : [20] And your _____ shall be spent in _____ : for your land shall not yield her increase, neither shall the trees of the land yield their fruits.

[21] And if ye walk _____ unto me, and will not hearken unto me; I will bring seven times more plagues upon you according to your sins. [22] I will also send wild beasts among you, which shall rob you of your _____ , and destroy your cattle, and make you few in number; and your high ways shall be desolate. [23] And if ye will not be _____ by me by these things, but will walk contrary unto me; [24] Then will I also walk contrary unto you, and will punish you yet seven times for your sins. [25] And I will bring a sword upon you, that shall avenge the quarrel of my covenant: and when ye are gathered together within your cities, I will send the pestilence among you; and ye shall be delivered into the hand of the enemy. [26] And when I have broken the staff of your bread, ten women shall bake your bread in one oven, and they shall deliver you your bread again by weight: and ye shall eat, and not be satisfied. [27] And if ye will not for all this hearken unto me, but walk contrary unto me; [28] Then I will walk contrary unto you also in _____ ; and I, even I, will _____ you seven times for your sins. [29] And ye shall eat the flesh of your sons, and the flesh of your daughters shall ye eat. [30] And I will _____ your high places, and cut down your _____ , and cast your _____ upon the carcases of your idols, and my soul shall abhor you. [31] And I will make your cities waste, and bring your sanctuaries unto desolation, and I will not smell the savour of your sweet odours. [32] And I will bring the land into _____ : and your enemies which dwell therein shall be _____ at it. [33] And I will _____ you among the _____ , and will draw out a sword after you: and your land shall be desolate, and your cities waste. [34] Then shall the land enjoy her sabbaths, as long as it lieth desolate, and ye be in your enemies' land; even then shall the land rest, and enjoy her sabbaths. [35] As long as it lieth desolate it shall rest; because it did not rest in your sabbaths, when ye dwelt upon it. [36] And upon them that are left alive of you I will send a _____ into their hearts in the lands of their enemies; and the sound of a shaken leaf shall _____ them; and they shall flee, as fleeing from a sword; and they shall fall when none pursueth. [37] And they shall fall one upon another, as it were before a sword, when none pursueth: and ye shall have no _____ to stand before your enemies. [38] And ye shall perish among the heathen, and the land of your enemies shall eat you up. [39] And they that are left of you shall _____ away in their iniquity in your enemies' lands; and also in the iniquities of their fathers shall they pine away with them. [40] If they shall _____ their

_____, and the iniquity of their fathers, with their _____ which they trespassed against me, and that also they have walked contrary unto me; [41] And that I also have walked contrary unto them, and have brought them into the land of their enemies; if then their uncircumcised hearts be humbled, and they then _____ of the _____ of their iniquity: [42] Then will I _____ my _____ with _____, and also my covenant with _____, and also my covenant with _____ will I remember; and I will _____ the _____. [43] The land also shall be left of them, and shall enjoy her sabbaths, while she lieth desolate without them: and they shall accept of the punishment of their iniquity: because, even because they despised my judgments, and because their soul abhorred my statutes. [44] And yet for all that, when they be in the land of their enemies, I will _____ cast them away, neither will I abhor them, to destroy them utterly, and to break my covenant with them: for I am the Lord their God. [45] But I will for their sakes _____ the _____ of their ancestors, whom I brought forth out of the land of Egypt in the sight of the heathen, that I might be their God: I am the Lord. [46] These are the statutes and judgments and laws, which the Lord made between him and the children of Israel in mount Sinai by the hand of Moses.

[27:1] And the Lord spake unto Moses, saying, [2] Speak unto the children of Israel, and say unto them, When a man shall make a singular _____, the persons shall be for the Lord by thy estimation. [3] And thy estimation shall be of the male from twenty years old even unto sixty years old, even thy estimation shall be fifty shekels of silver, after the shekel of the sanctuary. [4] And if it be a female, then thy estimation shall be thirty shekels. [5] And if it be from five years old even unto twenty years old, then thy estimation shall be of the male twenty shekels, and for the female ten shekels. [6] And if it be from a month old even unto five years old, then thy estimation shall be of the male five shekels of silver, and for the female thy estimation shall be three shekels of silver. [7] And if it be from sixty years old and above; if it be a male, then thy estimation shall be fifteen shekels, and for the female ten shekels. [8] But if he be poorer than thy estimation, then he shall present himself before the priest, and the priest shall value him; according to his ability that vowed shall the priest value him. [9] And if it be a beast, whereof men bring an offering unto the Lord, all that any man giveth of such unto the Lord shall be holy. [10] He shall not _____ it, nor _____ it, a _____ for a _____, or a _____ for a _____: and if he shall at all change beast for beast, then it and the exchange thereof shall be holy. [11] And if it be any unclean beast, of which they do not offer a sacrifice unto the Lord, then he shall present the beast before the priest: [12] And the priest shall value it, whether it be good or bad: as thou valuest it, who art the priest, so shall it be. [13] But if he will at all redeem it, then he shall _____ a _____ part thereof unto thy estimation.

[14] And when a man shall _____ his _____ to be _____ unto the Lord, then the priest shall estimate it, whether it be good or bad: as the priest shall estimate it, so shall it stand. [15] And if he that sanctified it will redeem his house, then he shall _____ the _____ part of the _____ of thy estimation unto it, and it shall be his. [16] And if a man shall _____ unto the Lord some part of a _____ of his possession, then thy estimation shall be according to the seed thereof: an homer of barley seed shall be valued at fifty shekels of silver. [17] If he _____ his _____ from the year of _____, according to thy

LEVITICUS

estimation it shall stand. [18] But if he sanctify his field _____ the _____, then the priest shall reckon unto him the money according to the years that remain, even unto the year of the jubile, and it shall be abated from thy estimation. [19] And if he that sanctified the field will in any wise redeem it, then he shall add the fifth part of the money of thy estimation unto it, and it shall be assured to him. [20] And if he will not redeem the field, or if he have sold the field to another man, it shall not be redeemed any more. [21] But the field, when it goeth out in the jubile, shall be holy unto the Lord, as a field devoted; the possession thereof shall be the priest's. [22] And if a man sanctify unto the Lord a field which he hath bought, which is not of the fields of his possession; [23] Then the priest shall reckon unto him the worth of thy estimation, even unto the year of the jubile: and he shall give thine estimation in that day, as a holy thing unto the Lord. [24] In the year of the jubile the field shall return unto him of whom it was bought, even to him to whom the possession of the land did belong. [25] And all thy estimations shall be according to the shekel of the sanctuary: twenty gerahs shall be the shekel.

[26] Only the firstling of the beasts, which should be the Lord's firstling, no man shall sanctify it; whether it be ox, or sheep: it is the Lord's. [27] And if it be of an unclean beast, then he shall redeem it according to thine estimation, and shall add a fifth part of it thereto: or if it be not redeemed, then it shall be sold according to thy estimation. [28] Notwithstanding no devoted thing, that a man shall devote unto the Lord of all that he hath, both of man and beast, and of the field of his possession, shall be sold or redeemed: every devoted thing is most holy unto the Lord. [29] None devoted, which shall be devoted of men, shall be redeemed; but shall surely be put to death. [30] And _____ the _____ of the _____, whether of the _____ of the land, or of the _____ of the tree, is the _____: it is _____ unto the _____. [31] And if a man will at all _____ ought of his _____, he shall _____ thereto the _____ part thereof. [32] And concerning the tithe of the herd, or of the flock, even of whatsoever passeth under the rod, the _____ shall be holy unto the Lord. [33] He shall not search whether it be good or bad, neither shall he change it: and if he change it at all, then both it and the change thereof shall be holy; it shall not be redeemed. [34] These are the commandments, which the Lord commanded Moses for the children of Israel in mount _____.

Made in United States
Troutdale, OR
04/05/2024

18968800R00022